MANAGING TO
BE DIFFERENT

MANAGING TO
BE DIFFERENT

Educational Leadership as
Critical Practice

R O N   S C A P P

Routledge
Taylor & Francis Group
New York   London

Routledge is an imprint of the
Taylor & Francis Group, an informa business

Published in 2006 by
Routledge
Taylor & Francis Group
270 Madison Avenue
New York, NY 10016

Published in Great Britain by
Routledge
Taylor & Francis Group
2 Park Square
Milton Park, Abingdon
Oxon OX14 4RN

Printed in the United States of America on acid-free paper
10 9 8 7 6 5 4 3 2 1

International Standard Book Number-10: 0-415-94862-2 (Hardcover) 0-415-94863-0 (Softcover)
International Standard Book Number-13: 978-0-415-94862-3 (Hardcover) 978-0-415-94863-0 (Softcover)
Library of Congress Card Number 2005027266

Library of Congress Cataloging-in-Publication Data

Scapp, Ron, 1955-
    Managing to be different : educational leadership as critical practice / Ron Scapp.
        p. cm.
    Includes bibliographical references and index.
    ISBN 0-415-94862-2 (hb : alk. paper) -- ISBN 0-415-94863-0 (pb : alk. paper) 1.
    Educational leadership--Social aspects--United States. 2. School management and
    organization--Social aspects--United States. 3. Critical pedagogy--United States. I.
    Title

LB2805.S316 2006
371.2--dc22

                                                     2005027266

Taylor & Francis Group
is the Academic Division of Informa plc.

Visit the Taylor & Francis Web site at
http://www.taylorandfrancis.com

and the Routledge Web site at
http://www.routledge-ny.com

For all those many awful meetings, the people who refused to listen, the really bad decisions that were made... and to all who have had to endure such leadership...

Note: The names have been changed to give the guilty at least one more chance.

CONTENTS

ACKNOWLEDGMENTS

Throughout the years I have had the good fortune of working with many different people, all of whom have taught me a great deal about integrity, generosity, and hope. They have taught me about managing to be different. I want to thank them all. I particularly want to express my gratitude and appreciation to my colleagues at the UFT/New York City Teacher Center: Aminda Gentile, director and Mary Diaz, assistant director have proven once again to be generous, supportive, and committed collaborators. I would also like to thank the entire planning committee of the UFT/Urban Educators Forum whose members create at unbelievable speed and quality. The committee members include: Catalina B. Fortino, Bea Carson, Mary Diaz, Jonathan Molofsky, Barbara Mylite, Mary Ann Jordan, Iris Cabral, and Teresa Mehrer. I would also like to thank Alex Molnar, James Fraser, and Susanna Corothers. I want to acknowledge the influence of Barbara Bowen and her vision for a different kind of union. The staff of Region 8 in Brooklyn deserves much praise for the quality of their work; thank you Linda Harris, Bob Gallagher, and Allison Sheenan. I am very thankful of Susan Apold's efforts to make a difference; many people are the beneficiaries of her good work. I would also like to mention the integrity and courage of Miles Barker who, despite fighting for his life, manages to continue caring for and serving others in many ways. Thanks go out to Ken Saltman and Robin Goodman. I want to thank Linda Delgado and Doug Baker for their support and many good deeds. I am especially indebted to Steven F. Kruger for his ongoing participation in leadership and guidance. Finally, I want to express my gratitude to Meryl Siegman—she knows why.

INTRODUCTION

The fact is that a man who wants to act virtuously in every way necessarily comes to grief among so many who are not virtuous. Therefore if a prince wants to maintain his rule he must learn how not to be virtuous, and to make use of this or not according to need.

Niccolo Machiavelli, *The Prince*

I believe in political action, yes. Any kind of political action. I believe in action, period. Whatever kind of action is necessary. When you hear me say "by any means necessary," I mean exactly that. I believe in anything that is necessary to correct unjust conditions — political, economic, social, physical, anything that's necessary. I believe in it — as long as it's intelligently directed and designed to get results.

Malcolm X, *The Militant Labor Forum*

Over the years there have been many books, from all corners, professing expertise on the subject of leadership. We have witnessed (and in most cases, have had to endure) an onslaught of books by "proven leaders." We have had books by self-aggrandizing corporate

CEOs who boast increases in stock value and market share. There are memoirs from former politicians of all stripes who rewrite history to justify and explain their decisions (or at least try to). Professional sports figures present us with "last place to first place" accounts while expounding the virtues of spelling — there is no "I" in "team." And we are offered inspired testimony by the heads of various religious groups espousing "the word" as only they can pronounce it. Basically, anyone able to lay claim to some sort of success — in this world or beyond — has published (typically in the "as-told-to" format) his or her philosophy of leadership. They do this, they claim, to help average individuals achieve their goals and to offer tips to other leaders who aspire to go, as bestselling author Jim Collins phrases it, from "good to great."

Interestingly enough, these how-to books and their philosophies have made a big impact on many different people and professional fields, including the field of education. From President Bush's "No Child Left Behind" initiative, to the University of Phoenix's "for profit" model of education for consumers on the go; from the hiring of former military personnel to head school districts, to the wholesale adoption of the corporate vocabulary and the credo of accountability, efficiency, and quality control, educational leadership has been handed over to those who can "make things happen." Lost in the discussion (as if there really ever was one) is the possibility that those who are committed to, as Paulo Freire frames it, "education as the practice of freedom" can contribute something of value. What seems consistently to win the day is celebrity leadership — leadership as self-promotion. Here, however, what will be discussed is educational leadership as critical practice; that is, leadership as the hard work of acknowledging, understanding, and responding to the power dynamics that exist in all institutions, including academia.

Managing to Be Different is not, therefore, a how-to book or a success story for all to read and try to repeat. It is, instead, part testimony, part analysis, and part entreaty. It is a book identifying and describing what I consider to be some important issues challenging those attempting to be different, challenging those attempting to engage in educational leadership as something other than merely running a tight ship or maintaining the status quo. This is an effort explicitly to address the fact that there are people who are administrators and who are committed to critical pedagogy, people who view educational leadership as critical practice.

A few years back we heard the laments and warnings from social conservatives and the religious right regarding the rise of, to use Roger Kimball's expression, "tenured radicals." Along with other conservative commentators (most notably William Bennett and Dinesh D'Souza), Kimball charged that there are too many radicals from the Sixties who have infiltrated the educational system, especially institutions of higher education. The argument claims that these radical educators have been corrupting the integrity and objectivity of academic endeavor — along with our nation's moral and cultural values — with political correctness, multiculturalism, feminism, and the epistemological relativism that comes with postmodernism.[1] For these conservatives and their political and religious allies, academia has fallen victim to the whims of progressives who are unpatriotic, trashing Western culture and promoting amoral lifestyles (read, demanding rights for lesbian, gay, and transgender citizens). It is my hope that *Managing to Be Different* will only add to their concern. I say this, however, not because I articulate anything that could be mistaken for a left-wing manifesto for would-be radical administrators, but rather due to my effort to call attention to the need for more administrators to participate in educational leadership as critical practice. That is, this book joins the task of educational administration with critical pedagogy and thereby presents such leadership *as nothing more but nothing less than serving the mission of teaching and learning in the spirit of education as the practice of freedom.* Thus, conservatives (inside as well as outside academia) might be angered still further by such a position.

In her well-argued book *Unruly Practices*, philosopher and social theorist Nancy Fraser notes that "[t]he real contradictions of our lives notwithstanding, the radical academic is not an oxymoron" (1). *Managing to Be Different* attempts to extend the merits of such a position by offering the reader a critical perspective on administrating from a radical stance, the contradictions notwithstanding — namely, supporting education as the practice on freedom. By using the work of Paulo Freire, Henry A. Giroux, and bell hooks, among others, as my foundation, instead of relying on the plethora of commercial books on leadership influenced by corporate, sports, military, and religious imagery and metaphors, I want to explore and discuss other dimensions of educational administration, aspects of educational leadership grounded in supporting teaching and learning, and in doing so with a critical eye. This means looking at how those of us who work at, or are otherwise connected to, educational institutions function, react, and perform with and against the power relations that do exist in and that, in many ways, define academia.

If some of you who see the term "academia" think that this book is only for those involved with institutions of higher education, you are right and wrong. You are correct to the degree that *Managing to Be Different* primarily (though certainly not exclusively) addresses power relations as I have experienced them throughout my career in higher education. You are mistaken, however, to the extent that you believe that educational leadership at the college or university level is of little importance or value to those who teach or work as administrators at elementary and secondary schools. I say this for a variety of reasons that I hope will be clearer as you read on. But for the moment, I want to emphasize two particular reasons why school principals, deans, chairs, guidance counselors, heads of programs, and classroom teachers should find this book to be of some pragmatic and theoretical significance.

I believe that my effort here should be of some interest and value to those not at institutions of higher education because:

1. Those who teach and administrate at the elementary and secondary school levels have come through higher education to get their credentials.
2. The issues covered in this book should be of concern for everyone thinking about leadership, power, administration, and teaching and learning.

In the first instance, I think it is important to remember that those of you who teach and administrate at the elementary and secondary school levels have worked your way through colleges and universities generally and teacher education programs specifically (one way or another).[2] Typically you then have gone on to earn advanced degrees, certification extensions, and supervisory credentials at institutions of higher education, more often than not coordinated or issued by a teacher education program or school of education. Knowing more about the power dynamics of educational institutions at this level lets you gain some additional insight about your own professional and personal education experience (as if they are separate). For example, why is it that your major or program, your department, and your discipline uses this particular model, book, strategy, or philosophy, and does not employ some other perspective or technique? Discussing and thinking about how your professors collaborate in order to put together a curriculum or program could reveal some important aspects (or biases?) regarding your own education and professional perspective. How often do we go back in order to reconsider and reevaluate our own body of knowledge or ask how did it come to gain currency and dominance?

Given the fact that much of what is discussed in this book focuses on commitment, power, generosity of spirit, community, and critical pedagogy, it strikes me that anyone interested in seriously thinking about (or rethinking) issues of leadership and education would find this a persuasive second reason for finding *Managing to Be Different* to be of interest. That the book does not specifically address what a high school assistant principal for administration should or should not do regarding an issue such as scheduling (important as this is) ought not to dissuade or discourage assistant principals from reading on. (By the way, there are many, many books — and even some good ones — about such matters.) This book is intended to push things in a different direction. In short, for those of you who are principals, supervisors, superintendents, and administrators with other titles, *Managing to Be Different* is written with the aim of presenting a "critical perspective" — that is, a viewpoint that might contribute to the process of provoking your own critical analysis of educational leadership.

It is, however, my goal to offer those in administrative positions at institutions of higher education a book not typically required or available for courses and workshops on educational leadership and administration. I mean this in three ways. First, I hope that those of you who are administrators will read this book and find in it situations and circumstances that you have had to deal with and confront discussed in a manner and from a perspective not widely published — a different kind of source book as it were. Second, for those who *are* committed to educational leadership as critical practice and who teach courses leading to the requisite certification for principals, supervisors, and superintendents, it is my aim to offer you a supplementary, if not quite complementary, book to be used in conjunction with the many other traditional books on educational leadership. Third, it is also my intention that those who are not administrators, especially younger and "junior" faculty, find this book of some help. I want to provide a different take on what those who are committed to educational leadership as critical practice are struggling against and struggling for. Perhaps most importantly, I hope that in reading this book, non-administrators will acknowledge the role that they can and must play in educational leadership — "leadership" is not just for administrators (they too often lack it anyway); it is for everyone engaged in the often hard but always vital work of critical pedagogy.

Managing to Be Different attempts to talk differently about administration. It lays out a number of issues, circumstances and dynamics that are at play at educational institutions of all types and argues that a fundamental understanding of the dynamics of power is essential to all involved in education as the practice of freedom. But as Thomas J. Sergiovanni points out in his thoughtful and useful book, *Moral Leadership*:

> This kind of talk — about attitudes and values informing our leadership practice; about how visions, for better and for worse, frame our views and the views of others; about leadership's belonging to everyone; about the placement of content and substance (teaching and learning, building learning communities) over process and skills — is a new kind of leadership talk. It represents the voice of practice, a voice largely neglected in the traditional school-leadership literature. (1)

Managing to Be Different is very much about "this kind of talk." By identifying and discussing what I take to be a practice oriented perspective (in the sense of actually *being* different), this book strives to bring the focus of leadership back to a particular type of practice, namely education as the practice of freedom.

Some might object that the simple act of identifying a method, in this case following Paulo Freire's use of "dialogue" to engage in education as the practice of freedom, runs the risk of merely jumping on the methodology bandwagon of the moment. For example, many people these days disingenuously evoke Freire's commitment to dialogue but, in fact, only pay lip service to such mutual exchange. In institutions of education across the United States today, we have people in the name of dialogue actually working against the real political possibilities generated by genuine dialogical exchange. As Donaldo Macedo argues in his important book, *Literacies of Power*, many have appropriated the "dialogical method" and have engaged in very little actual dialogue. Macedo tells us:

The appropriation of the dialogical method as a process of sharing experiences is often reduced to a form of group therapy that focuses on the psychology of the individual. Although some educators may claim that this process creates a pedagogical comfort zone, in my view, it does little beyond making the oppressed feel good about his or her own sense of victimization. In other words, the sharing of experiences should not be understood in psychological terms only. It invariably requires a political and ideological analysis as well. That is the sharing of experiences must always be understood within a social praxis that entails both reflection and political action. In short, it must always involve a political project with the objective of dismantling oppressive structures and mechanisms. (175)

It is my goal to present to the reader such an effort. Managing to Be Different attempts to offer the reader the type of "political and ideological analysis" that Macedo rightly demands. Throughout the book I try to engage in the sort of reflection and discussion that lead to, if not demonstrate, some possibilities of (political) action, however modest. From my perspective managing to be different is an ongoing social and cultural struggle and, therefore, is a political act. Of course, sustaining such a struggle — that is, managing to remain different over time — requires a great deal of individual effort and a commitment to working with others. It involves continuously asking the question, How might we come to see differently the ways that power relations in academia unfold, the way they are maintained, the way they can be challenged, and the way they can be altered? Such questioning is educational leadership as critical practice. It is the purpose of this book to bring this practice to the attention of those in administrative positions, and to bring to their attention the practice of critically engaging in leadership, as opposed to merely managing a department, program, or school.

I have tried to identify some of the issues and circumstances that strike me as important for participating in education as the practice of freedom. I analyze and discuss themes, ideas, and situations that are not unique to educational institutions but do have a particularly "academic" quality about them. By referring to the work of such diverse thinkers, critics, and commentators as the sociologist Pierre Bourdieu; cultural theorists bell hooks, Gayatri Chakravorty Spivak, and Henry A. Giroux; and theater director Augusto Boal, among others, it is my desire to integrate their insights, criticisms, and experiences directly and specifically with a discussion about educational leadership and administration. I wanted there to be a different kind of book on a topic that seems more and more in the control of those who see educational leadership as anything but critical practice.

Managing to Be Different, then, attempts to do what Peter McLaren powerfully argues for in his book *Critical Pedagogy and Predatory Culture*; it

> attempts to analyze and unsettle extant power configurations, to defamiliarize and make remarkable what is often passed off as the ordinary, the mundane, the routine, the banal. In other words, [this book] ambiguates the complacency of teaching under the sign of modernity, that is, under a sign in which knowledge is approached as ahistorical and neutral and separated from value and power. (231)

Managing to Be Different is an effort to continue to extend the work of critical pedagogy — namely, to break away from those givens that have dominated educational institutions, and worked against education as the practice of freedom. In this case, it is an effort explicitly to analyze and discuss, from a critical perspective, a domain of educational practice that has become part of what Macedo identifies as the "oppressive structures and mechanisms" at work in institutions of education.

In this sense, educational leadership is simultaneously an individual responsibility and effort and a political project involving the different communities who participate in critical practice. This means that while leadership emanates from an individual's commitment and willingness to take risks, it should not be reduced to one individual per se. Too many models of leadership employ a top-down (oppositional) relationship that demands an individual to lead (read, control, order, or require) others to perform particular tasks. Such a view of leadership usually conflates expertise and authority with authoritarian rule, the kind that is typical in corporate, military, sports, and religious paradigms. But even those who do not subscribe to these kinds of models can also too easily limit leadership to "the leader." The problem arises not so much from recognizing an individual's ability, skill, and talent as from the act of burdening that individual with leading all others. In addition, in the process of recognizing only one individual, we fail to acknowledge that many others, not singled out, can and must participate in leadership. In short, leadership is as much about communities and multiplicity as it is about the individual.

If we consider for a moment the often-quoted phrase "No one is indispensable," perhaps we can gain some insight into the workings of many organizations. Unfortunately, this phrase is typically asserted when someone speaks up, makes a demand or challenges the dominant view (and is being threatened with being fired or demoted). It is usually a cynical statement about the ultimate value of an individual's contribution to an institution, group, or team. But if we take a slightly different perspective and say, "OK,

no one is indispensable; however, *everyone* can make a difference," then we begin to see how leadership is at the same time an
individual responsibility and a shared effort. Of course, there will
inevitably emerge some dynamic individuals who at a particular
moment serve a more prominent role and will have more to offer.
Still, everyone can make a difference: leadership is about everyone participating in the responsibility of being engaged in creating and sustaining an environment that best serves education as
the practice of freedom.

Educational leadership as critical practice presumes and
requires a different dynamic than the top-down, leader-follower
structure. It seeks something more like what the French philosopher Gilles Deleuze and psychoanalyst Felix Guattari describe,
in their magnificently original book *A Thousand Plateaus*, as
"rhizomatic." That is, it is a dynamic that involves spreading
and multiplying power — not reducing it to some one individual designated or identified as the starting point (of action) or
some others identified as the finish line (of completing the task).
Educational leadership as critical practice is always in the middle
of things — considering, reconsidering, and moving on *with* others, not dictating, disciplining, and simply reproducing the status
quo.

This is why genuine educational leadership is encountered
through the multiplicity of engagements and interactions that
an educational institution *as* community (or more accurately as
communities) can and must support and sustain. This is opposed
to a notion of educational leadership as engaged in directing or
managing others to "deliver" or "supply" educational services or
products (courses) to students who, in this model, are understood
as consumers. Real leadership is about managing to be different.

The communities that participate in leadership as critical practice are doing so by dint of their individual commitment to teaching and learning and to social justice (close-at-hand and elsewhere). They are not merely responding to an edict announced by someone in charge telling everyone else to produce a qualified workforce, as defined by the dictates (the needs) of corporate globalization. They are, instead, compelled to lead the way toward education as the practice of freedom, because of who they are and what they believe.

This model, this undertaking, of leadership and the educational dynamics that flow from it demands a different image of leadership than what typically gets the attention of most administrators, politicians, alleged experts on leadership, and the various media that seemingly are forever searching for the next savior of education. As Thomas J. Sergiovanni notes:

> Establishing community norms within the school can serve as a substitute for direct leadership. Doing so involves changing the metaphor for schooling: from the image of an instructional delivery system, a factory, batch processing, an organization, a clinical setting, a market, or a garden to that of a *community*. Metaphors are important, for they frame the way we think about managing, leading, and schooling, and they create the reality that we ultimately live as school leaders. (45) [emphasis in original]

That is, establishing the networks of agency and activity that allow communities to participate in education as the practice of freedom requires a shift in the paradigm of leadership — from leader as sole source of power to communities of participation leading the way. Here, leadership is found everywhere within an educational institution and not just in the president's office, behind the provost's desk, or at a chairs' meeting. We must break away from the notion that overseeing and running things are synonymous with leadership. True, we really do need bureaucratic functionaries, but we also really need communities of leadership — those who have vision and commitment — if we are going to create and sustain something worthy of housing in educational institutions, namely education as the practice of freedom.

With this perspective on leadership we see it as more porous, amorphous, and widespread — that is, not limited to or limited by just one leader or dominant group. As just mentioned above, this does not mean that we do away with chairs, deans, directors, and others with administrative titles and responsibilities, but that the concept of leadership is extended beyond those traditional locations of authority. (By the way, it is truly a great thing when someone in such a position actually participates in leadership.) Those who make up the different communities of participation must begin to see themselves as the forces that enact education as the practice of freedom, and not rely on being told, assigned, or appointed the task of doing something different. *Managing to Be Different* offers some reflections and strategies on how "to analyze and unsettle extant power configurations," as Peter McLaren put it. But as I have already indicated (see page 3), it is by no means intended to be a new and improved how-to book, but a book that provokes critical thoughts and responses to shared situations and concerns.

In presenting the topics and themes of the following chapters it is my goal to begin a genuine dialogue on educational administration that accepts and engages a role for leadership that transgresses the established (power) lines of demarcation — that is, a dialogue about leadership as critical practice. I am in no way assuming that any of this translates directly into some kind of desktop reference book. I do hold out the hope, however, that thinking about some of these things from a different perspective might persuade those in administrative positions, as well as those who are not, to try managing to be different.

1

WHO, ME? AN ADMINISTRATOR?

In the late 1970s I had the good fortune to work at LaGuardia Community College in Long Island City (L.I.C.), an industrial neighborhood just at the base of the Queens side of the 59th Street Bridge (the Queensborough Bridge). At the time, the area was a mixture of New York's manufacturing past and its future as a center for technology, design, and the arts. In many ways, LaGuardia Community College represented the city's transition from a major manufacturing locus into a new urban identity yet to be fully determined. It was a place of dynamic commercial and creative energy; it was also a place I knew well.

Since grammar school my friends and I roamed the streets of L.I.C. by bicycle and on foot because of its intrinsic appeal to us: railroad tracks, active and abandoned factories, cobblestone streets, access to the East River and Newton Creek, views of the Manhattan skyline, "old man" bars and a general sense that this was simultaneously one of the most artificial and natural places ever developed or inhabited.

LaGuardia Community College was originally sandwiched between a paper factory and a gum manufacturer. Farther east on Thomson Avenue there were the railroad yards and the freight trains that continuously moved goods of all sorts in and out of New York. Despite the fact that at the time the city was suffering from various local financial blunders and national economic setbacks, New York was still its ever-frenetic self. It was an edgy time, and L.I.C. was an edgy place. LaGuardia Community College was part of the undetermined future of this neighborhood, and its students, faculty, and staff were all part of the mix.

I began working as a tutor, specifically a literacy tutor. LaGuardia had a large and well-organized basic skills program with math, English, and reading components. The remedial courses offered through these different departments were a response to the combination of Vietnam vets coming back to or starting school with government monies, recent immigrants who were taking advantage of the full array of useful courses at LaGuardia, and "traditional" students seeking to work their way through a community college en route to a bachelor's degree from one of the many four-year colleges in New York, but who could not go directly to such a college. LaGuardia was (and remains) an urban, multicultural, and intergenerational population striving to improve its understanding of the world, as well as its social and economic status. The faculty and staff at the college were a committed group of educators and administrators attempting to facilitate the teaching and learning that students sought at LaGuardia. I found myself amidst a community of diverse, hardworking, and ambitious people, a community that was transforming the city as much as it was transforming itself.

In 1979 I had been working at LaGuardia Community College for about four years. In June of that year I also finished my own undergraduate education and was thinking seriously about graduate school but hadn't yet applied or even thoroughly investigated where I might go to pursue my studies. Although I had some overall sense of my future plans, upon graduation I found myself without an immediate next step to take. An interesting opportunity arose, however, and an unanticipated path was laid out before me. I was offered a full-time position as a master tutor-counselor; it was a hybrid position, part pedagogue and part administrator. One would think that someone fresh out of college, interested in a career as an educator and comfortable with his work and his colleagues at LaGuardia, would have jumped at the chance for a full-time academic job. Oddly enough, I didn't. The reason for my hesitation seems, in retrospect, a bit immature, if not foolish.

Prior to the job offer, I had seen myself solely as a tutor. I had successfully developed relationships with students that proved effective in helping them raise their reading levels, and I also genuinely enjoyed the one-to-one tutoring and the group tutoring I was originally hired to do. I saw myself as a novice teacher, someone engaged with those who were learning and discovering things about themselves and the world at large, someone who was learning and discovering things about himself and the world, in large measure because of the students I served. I felt a sense of pride. I was proud of the direct and immediate role I played in the lives of the students of LaGuardia and I had little desire to disrupt or forfeit that dynamic, especially by becoming an administrator.

True, it was 1979, and the Sixties — even by a loose chronology — had long ago ended, but the thought of becoming an administrator — that is to say, part of the managing system — was hard for me to embrace. Naively, I found the prospect of joining the ranks of the institution's establishment unappealing at best and prima facie somewhat hypocritical at worst. Wrongly, I took it as a given that administrators were the ones who made everything complicated and dogmatic, that people who wanted to really change things and help others had to stay clear of everything bureaucratic and connected with those "in charge." As one could imagine, it was with a great deal of trepidation that I considered the offer. But consider it I did, and my sense of academic engagement was forever influenced by my choice to take the position. And though my initial hesitation to become an administrator was based on a flawed understanding, my experience, in many ways, proved even more daunting.

Almost as soon as I accepted the position, I learned my first important lesson: one cannot ignore workplace history. Although I had agreed to take a newly created position — a position with ostensibly no history — I encountered numerous people informing me of the history of the position, of my position. I was told why I was chosen and what problems lay ahead for me given the existing power structure, and I was informed about those people I needed to make peace with, if I ever hoped to be effective doing my job. (There were, it seems, more than just a few others considered for the job. Unbeknownst to me, one person in particular was viewed as the insider. This person, in fact, had been at LaGuardia much longer than I, and had made genuine contributions to the tutoring program. It turns out that this other tutor had even been part of the process of coming up with the job description for the position. In addition to people having different favorites, the very nature and purpose of the job was evidently being debated up until the last moment.) Within days, I was confronted by years of distrust, frustration, and disappointment at varying levels of intensity and consequence. The very same place I had come to know as a source of satisfaction and achievement was overnight transformed into a complicated and vexed field of political struggle. The new position I occupied quickly revealed itself to be an always already contested location; I immediately became a politico-historical focus of attention. I was now differently situated within the existing power dynamics of the institution. Who approached me and how they did so were, to my surprise, almost always predetermined by events and exchanges that occurred before, in some cases long before, my being hired. But all of that history, from my appointment forward, was to be somehow identified with me.

It is not so much the case that everyone assigned a direct causal link between me and the feuds and problems of the past; it was something more complicated and, at the same time, more simple than that. For reasons both understandable and far-fetched, I automatically (and as I later on understood, axiomatically) became a hot spot on the institutional power grid. It wasn't really about me, as such, but rather it was very much about that which was all around me, perhaps, more accurately, about all that which now ran through me. The moment I accepted the position, I became part of the circuitry of power, part of the surges, breaks, and relays of the institution, in a fashion not previously possible. Just by being inserted into the network in this manner, I was instantaneously connected to (and confronted by) the swirls of forces that characterize, and too often determine, much of what happens in institutions of all stripes, but certainly in higher education. The charged field was impossible to ignore, no less deny, yet the range of acknowledgment concerning its existence, the various modes of participation in it, and the different struggles underway by those seeking the status bestowed by it were neither straightforward nor always comprehensible, given the order of things. In short, not much made sense, at least at first.

In a relatively short time, I began to see, hear, and understand things in a different way. People said things they did not mean; they often did not say the things they did mean; they supported people they adamantly disagreed with; and they voted against proposals and people they claimed elsewhere to support. A small gesture such as nodding in agreement or not voicing an objection at a meeting concerning an otherwise innocuous issue could be taken as loud public endorsement. It could be seen as a move to mend old wounds, or that same gesture could be understood as an absolute betrayal of trust and an attack on someone's credibility or value. Those in attendance, those who witnessed the said gesture, if prodded, could provide you with the history, the context, the significance of the "yes" or silence, of the "perhaps" or the "I am not sure." As I learned, the power field is always charged. Saying hello or not noticing someone because you continued to read your newspaper while you were eating your lunch in the cafeteria could trigger speculation, emotional distress, and relief. Anything could set off a reaction; no place was neutral within the grid. Static was everywhere.

I was twenty-four years old and, until this job, felt mature. The fact is, I had not experienced such an expression of problems and issues in my prior working life. I had been working since I was a kid. From delivering papers to working behind the counter at a neighborhood candy shop, from hauling groceries to being an hourly worker at a national supermarket chain, I had witnessed and been part of a variety of power plays and games. But I never encountered anything quite like what transpired at LaGuardia. I had been party to or had suffered from a host of power dynamics before accepting my position as an administrator. They were the typical sorts of things: covering for people who were late; working harder to compensate for someone who was ill but could not afford to take time off; enduring bad moods and abuse from a boss who was in turn being abused; and trying to keep the peace between coworkers who hated each other. But none of this prepared me for what I was to encounter in my new position. I became afraid of electrifying myself or someone else by accidentally blinking, sneezing, or coughing at the wrong moment. I was forced to learn the history of things such as they were. The questions, of course, were how to learn this history and from whom, and what to do with what one learned.

As I have just suggested, one of the most interesting, perhaps profound, aspects of being plugged into the circuitry — even if in a minor role — is the fact that so much passes through you. (On another important [paradoxical] level it should also be noted how much typically gets rerouted or bypassed around individual circuits at particular moments.) What I want to emphasize here is the following point: if one is inserted, placed, or otherwise installed in the right position, and if this is done in the proper manner, it is virtually impossible *not* to be connected to other relays in the system. In short, it is not really an option to disconnect oneself, not to be part of the conductivity, without unplugging or removing oneself from the whole system — not an easy task. You can miss a meeting or two, but hiding is, at best, a short-lived strategy. However far-removed from the source of power or a given surge, regardless of how roundabout the route, each relay, each breaker serves a purpose, is in fact institutionally necessary to guarantee connectivity, if only for a particular moment. One's circuitous function, then, is ultimately just as much a given in such a system as it is a consequence.

Within a year this circuitous function drove me from my job. I believe I might have stayed on longer, but I was accepted into a doctoral program in philosophy and decided to pull myself out. I did not exactly run from LaGuardia; I did, however, make a fairly quick exit. The process of learning about the circuitry, including the mistakes, the wrong moves, and the various malfunctions, convinced me that I would never again be an administrator. I wrongly assumed that unplugging oneself from administrating unplugged one from the circuitry. It would be quite some time before I realized that any connection to the power grid establishes conductivity. When I left LaGuardia, I simply assumed I was done with such matters. The truth, of course, was very different; I had only experienced my first conscious engagement with power and academia.

It is not that I had not experienced the relationship between power and education before LaGuardia; I had. Throughout my school life I had encountered many instances of power. From being removed from class to participating in an ongoing dialogue on racism in high school, from being part of student government to helping establish a successful mini-school (see *The Learning Community* by James Penha and John Azrak), it is fair to say that I experienced and understood something about the nature of power dynamics in education. I was, however, unaware of education as a professional arena — that is, unaware of academia. It wasn't until my employment (deployment?) at LaGuardia that a whole new dimension of power revealed itself and made its impact upon me.

In many ways I was frightened by my position at LaGuardia and I genuinely suspect that it was fear, more than anything else, that made me leave. I do not say this without some lingering embarrassment, but it is the case that I was scared. I was frightened by different things but was most worried about becoming someone or something I did not wish to become, namely an administrator. As I mentioned previously, I thought of myself as an educator, a facilitator of learning, not as part of the network of institutional power. At LaGuardia, I was frightened by the prospect of failing to remain engaged with students and colleagues in a creative and politically open manner. I assumed that becoming an administrator would, by definition, alter the nature of my relationships and turn me away from teaching. I incorrectly equated being an administrator with being an adminis*traitor*.

Regardless of how naïve or immature my assessment of the nature of things was, this is how I did in fact see things. For me everything creative and liberating was associated with teaching and learning; administrating was something that others, who could not or should not teach, did instead. This attitude emanated from a number of different sources, one of which was the desire to study and do philosophy. At the time my interest in philosophy, based on an aesthetic as well as an ethical impulse, made me hesitant to become part of the machinery of an institution, part of the controlling and limiting forces at work defining and deploying ways of being that intellectually and instinctively went counter to my own attempts to be different. As I saw it, there wasn't much difference, if any, between being an administrator and being a representative of bureaucracy in general. I imagined myself otherwise. I was part of a movement away from monitoring and disciplining and part of a larger cultural effort to support and assist others in the continuing struggle for social justice, a struggle that took place in classrooms and on the streets but not in offices. The years and experiences prior to my entering academia had influenced me away from the offices that housed administrators and managers and toward those who occupied the classrooms. My disposition was contrary to that of the position I was offered. I was temperamentally the wrong guy in the wrong place at the wrong time.

The French sociologist Pierre Bourdieu makes much of this notion of "disposition" and one's inclination to act or behave one way or another in different settings and circumstances. In his introduction to Bourdieu's *Language and Symbolic Power*, John B. Thompson describes the notion of disposition in the following way:

> Dispositions are acquired through a gradual process of inculcation in which early childhood experiences are particularly important. Through a myriad of mundane processes of training and learning, such as those involved in the inculcation of table manners ('sit up straight,' 'don't eat with your mouth full,' etc.), the individual acquires a set of dispositions which literally mould the body and become second nature. The dispositions produced thereby are also structured in the sense that they unavoidably reflect the social conditions within which they were acquired. An individual from a working-class background, for instance, will have acquired dispositions which are different in certain respects from those acquired by individuals who were brought up in a middle-class milieu. (Bourdieu, 13)

Whether you consider Bourdieu's perspective a wrongheaded throwback to Marx and Freud, or see his work as fundamental to understanding contemporary social practices, I want to emphasize the notion that my disposition(s) played an important role in my engagement as an administrator and my decision to quit. Who you are (however that may be defined or explained) determines how you are — how you act, negotiate, respond, and so on. The ways in which you have come to work your way through circumstances and situations make an imprint on you as well as the world around you. Your way of responding, your strategies, and even the way you move your body are not just actions, but expressions of a certain way of being. Cumulatively over time, these expressions of who you are, *are* your history, your lasting mark on the world, others, and yourself. Facile as it may sound, who you have been becoming endures. As Thompson notes:

> Structured dispositions are also durable: they are ingrained in the body in such a way that they endure through the life history of the individual, operating in a way that is pre-conscious and hence not readily amenable to conscious reflection and modification. Finally, the dispositions are generative and transposable in the sense that they are capable of generating a multiplicity of practices and perceptions in fields other than those in which they were originally acquired. (13)

In this sense, who we have been — how our bodies have been molded — influences how we will be, how we will act.

Such a perspective, however, should not be understood as endorsing a strict or narrow sense of determining how one becomes who one is. Instead, the reference to Bourdieu should be taken as useful description. By this I mean that, in my opinion, Bourdieu's notion of disposition helps us better understand the various ways people from different backgrounds behave in power struggles — that is to say, how they behave within different power grids. It is in the rich and complex context of social attitudes (dispositions) and practices (not fixed rules) which evolve over time that, according to Bourdieu, inform (not predetermine) our actions and reactions. Beyond the analysis and description of what is commonly called character, typically evoked by those claiming to articulate and identify leadership qualities and other aspects of behavior, Bourdieu's work extends our understanding of the fullness and texture of one's inclinations and propensities based on the intricate and complicated range of one's lived experience. As I mentioned in the introduction, throughout this book I will continue to make use of Bourdieu, and others, in order to suggest different ways of thinking about and responding to power in general and specifically within an academic setting — that is, to suggest ways of managing to be different.

When I left LaGuardia, I was convinced that I would not need to think ever again about being an administrator or manager. I would teach and do my thing (write, present papers, etc.), leaving all the other stuff to somebody else, *anybody* else actually. It wasn't that my life as a lower-level administrator was horrible; clearly people around the world have endured genuine hardships far greater than being anxious about stepping on the toes or incurring the wrath of an irate academic. Yet it was not what I thought that I wanted to do. To evoke Herman Melville's Bartleby, I preferred not to. But as fate would have it ...

Upon completing (defending) my dissertation, I was offered a job. Unfortunately, it was an administrative position — I know, somehow this is all too familiar. This time around, however, there was no great internal debate as to whether or not I would take the position. I had just finished a Ph.D. in philosophy and wanted very much to stay in New York City — my taking the job was never really in doubt. But I was in even more of a state of existential uneasiness about becoming an administrator. Last time, I was a novitiate, a newcomer to the profession of academia, and I had a sense that the future was open, that I would one day be a teacher, far removed from the politics of administrating. Now I was much more aware of what it meant to be an administrator and not a professor. I had witnessed fellow graduate students uproot their lives (in many cases including the lives of their families) to take a teaching position, even a temporary non-tenure-track position. Too much energy and sacrifice had gone into earning the degree, too many years of just getting by and foregoing full-time employment in order to become a teacher. It is understandable, therefore, that one felt pressure to get a teaching job, regardless of where or for how long. There was something necessary about getting hired and being able to tell oneself as well as others that "I got a position."

In some ways I was both lucky and unlucky. Whereas others went through the time-consuming (and too often frustrating) process of looking for jobs, soliciting letters of recommendation, and seeking advice from just about anyone who would offer some, I knew, in advance, that I was staying put in New York and therefore would not be getting a teaching job anytime soon. I didn't even bother going on the job market, getting letters of recommendation, or discussing things with my advisors; there really wasn't any point. Why waste their time or mine with the outrageous goal of getting hired in New York City, in philosophy. I was emotionally prepared for being unable to say, "I got a position," and I was professionally prepared to do something other than teach philosophy in order to earn a living.

I think part of the reason that I was ready to forego even looking for a teaching position, besides my personal commitment to staying in New York for family reasons, was the fact that part of me felt the need to do something other than teach, if only for a little while. In addition to doing other things during the course of my graduate studies, I had been an adjunct instructor for a number of years at different institutions. As is true for many who are adjuncts, I worked very hard, doing a lot of additional work outside the classroom. I eventually suffered from what I call "adjunctivitis," a labor disease with many noticeable symptoms which affects everyone, not just the part-time instructor: ultimately, students, colleagues (full- and part-time), and the entire institution suffer from the dedicated, hard-working, overextended, individual efforts of the adjunct. Oddly enough, then, I was ready for a break from (such) teaching — even before I was ever hired as a full-time faculty member I needed a breather. It was within this vexed and perplexed moment that I was offered another opportunity to become an administrator.

Despite my more informed existential concerns about being an administrator, again, it was my experience at LaGuardia Community College that actually motivated me to try once more. While it might seem a bit contradictory, LaGuardia was a lot more than merely difficult or negative. True, as I have already mentioned, I left partly out of being frightened by the dynamics, but, even then, I realized that there were possibilities to do things and influence procedure and policy. Even in my short-lived role as an administrator there, I made an impact. Working with other administrators, instructors, students, and tutors, I helped reorganize lessons, offered more time slots for testing and retesting, and contributed to a more welcoming environment for all who entered the reading lab. Because of this other side to LaGuardia and my experiences during graduate school, I approached the new position as perhaps a once in a lifetime chance to see if doing things differently was a real possibility. I was determined to experiment and explore power relations with the purpose of better serving and encouraging others to be different. I decided to view my work as an opportunity to consider what might happen if one were committed to being different, to challenging and confronting the obstacles and embracing the possibilities. It wasn't just about this job or position; it was my first genuine effort to make academic work a critical practice. It was, as I saw it, part of a larger effort to challenge ideologically dogmatic positions and join those Henry A. Giroux, in his book *Impure Acts,* acknowledges "are breaking down the boundaries between academic life and public politics" (15).

LaGuardia was my first conscious encounter with power in academia; it has made a lasting impression on me. Since then I have had the opportunity to pursue teaching and administrating and have come to understand the importance of real, meaningful leadership for both. As I write about working and struggling as an administrator I know that my experience at LaGuardia was my introduction to the need to engage in a critical practice regarding both teaching and administrating. In my book *Teaching Values: Critical Perspectives on Education, Politics and Culture,* I try to identify some salient issues and alternative perspectives and strategies at stake for and available to those teaching in this current age of uncertainty. In this book I am attempting explicitly to address the issue of educational leadership as critical practice for administrators. First at LaGuardia and time and again since, I have met many administrators (and teachers) who have either forfeited or botched the struggle to reclaim, as Paulo Freire asserts, "education as the practice of freedom" (see *Education for Critical*

Consciousness, 1-59). Years of bitter fighting over education have confused and confounded this goal. As Giroux observes:

> Lost in these debates is a view of the university that demands reinvigorated notions of civic courage and action that address what it means to make teaching and learning more socially conscious and politically responsive in a time of growing conservatism, racism, and corporatism. (17)

It was my desire to be part of the effort to reinvigorate "civic courage and action" that convinced me to reenter academia with a critical perspective and a determination to be different. LaGuardia Community College gave me my first taste of what it would take to succeed or fail. One could always try to play it safe and attempt to stay at a safe distance, but LaGuardia taught me that there is no such neutral place. If you're in it, you're in it for real. It may have taken a number of years after I left LaGuardia, but I realized that I was in it, and in it for real. That I am in it as administrator may no longer surprise me, yet part of me still defiantly asks, "Who, me? An administrator?"

2

ACADEMIA AND THE
IDEOLOGY OF FATALISM

Like teaching, administrating can look different and, at times, can really be different. There is, however, a price to pay. In the simplest terms: messing with things can cost. It can cost time, emotional energy, promotions, and even the very support of those students and colleagues who are benefiting from your efforts. Part of the reason why so many administrators quickly return to business as usual, if they ever bother attempting to do things otherwise, is due to the inevitable flack they get — from all corners. If one is willing and actually able to disrupt the status quo then one must be ready for the fallout. Once you start undoing the order of things, people start reacting, nervously and negatively, even if they are the beneficiaries of your attempt to do things differently.

In the previous chapter I commented on the particular way in which I felt plugged in and connected to the circuitry of power at an educational institution. I also noted that attempting to disconnect oneself from the power grid was virtually impossible — leaving the institution might be the only way. Clearly, many "choose" this route. They drop out, resign, or find themselves forced to go elsewhere: sometimes temporarily (as a visiting professor or the recipient of a grant, sabbatical, or leave of absence) and sometimes permanently (being denied tenure, for example). In my case, the fear of becoming someone I did not wish to be propelled me away from a good place. I wasn't fully prepared — intellectually, politically, or emotionally — to do the necessary work and handle the consequences; I was frightened and so I left. Yes, I did return, but only after coming to terms with the nature of the work ahead of me: in making a genuine commitment to being different, I found the courage to be different. I stopped being intimidated. I got frightened (and still do) but refused to be scared off.

Unfortunately, too many in academia who do remain, even those ostensibly in positions of power, live and work in what Parker J. Palmer rightly identifies as "a culture of fear." This culture of fear has the perverse impact of rendering many of us who stay in academia *spiritually* disconnected (Palmer's emphasis) from the work we should be doing and the people we ought to be serving better. Oddly enough, we find ourselves somehow connected to the circuitry of power in a way that leaves us disconnected from each other and ourselves.

Palmer describes this existential condition in his book, *The Courage to Teach: Exploring the Inner Landscape of a Teacher's Life*:

If we want to develop and deepen the capacity for connected-
ness at the heart of good teaching, we must understand — and
resist — the perverse but powerful draw of the "disconnected"
life. How, and why, does academic culture discourage us from
living connected lives? How and why, does it encourage us
to distance ourselves from our students and our subjects, to
teach and learn at some remove from our own hearts?

On the surface, the answer seems obvious: we are distanced
by a grading system that separates teachers from students,
by departments that fragment fields of knowledge, by competition that makes students and teachers alike wary of their
peers, and by a bureaucracy that puts faculty and administration at odds.

Educational institutions are full of divisive structures, of
course, but blaming them for our brokenness perpetuates the
myth that the outer world is more powerful than the inner. The
external structures of education would not have the power to
divide us as they do if they were not rooted in one of the most
compelling features of our inner landscape — fear. (35-36)

It is this giving in to fear that, according to Palmer, diminishes
our relationships with students and colleagues and lessens our
capacity to challenge critically those "divisive structures" that too
often define academic life. Although Palmer is focusing on teaching, the importance of his observations can clearly be applied to
administrating: fear, far too often, characterizes the actions and
reactions of those in charge, and perpetuates the forces at work
undermining good administrating. If one messes with these
forces, look out. Just as Palmer asserts that we need "the courage to teach," it is equally true that we need to acknowledge that
the courage to engage in educational administration as a critical
practice is often lacking — absent due to fear.

Of course, it is understandable to be hesitant to do or say anything that could jeopardize one's job. But too often it is the fear of doing things differently and "messing up" — especially in a culture where change is typically viewed with suspicion — that prevents people from engaging in the very work they want and need to do. There is, however, a significant difference between hesitating and being frozen by fear. I believe that if one is honest, it is fairly easy to recall an instance when either you or a colleague has been frozen by fear. During the course of a career, in just about any field, there is at least one moment — if not numerous moments — that could or has put your professional life in jeopardy. Most of us, justifiably, weigh the risks (the possible harmful consequences), as we see them at the time; then we wait in order to see who might be first (other than ourselves) to challenge the problematic issue or decision. Typically, most people balk — that is, they freeze up; they say and do nothing (sometimes "sneaking by," sometimes not). As a result, the momentum, the movement, remains with the dominating individual or group. Those who dominate exercise their (uncontested) power, once again, which only reinforces the misperception that the dominant forces are unchallengeable. Even individuals who enjoy a privileged and protected status, and would not really suffer from speaking up, often refrain from doing so, if there is a chance of damaging or downgrading their privileged station: the fear of losing one's privilege can prove quite paralyzing. This, in part, helps to explain the frustrating phenomenon of why people in comfortable positions refuse to move, to act on the behalf of a cause or a colleague they support. For many, too many, it appears to be the case that there is a begrudging acceptance of how things are, and a collateral fear that prevents them from doing much about anything.

Paulo Freire laments this acquiescence in his *Pedagogy of Freedom: Ethics, Democracy and Civic Courage*:

> There is a lot of fatalism around us. An immobilizing ideology of fatalism, with its flighty postmodern pragmatism, which insists that we can do nothing to change the march of social-historical and cultural reality because this is how the world is anyway. (26-27)[1]

We have all witnessed, if not participated in, this "immobilizing ideology of fatalism" every time someone is wrongly denied tenure or a promotion or has something they have developed taken away from them or their students (for example, the questionable closing of a vibrant, albeit unorthodox, program). Because so many have fallen under the spell of "this is how the world is anyway," too much goes unchallenged and too little gets changed.

But as Freire rightly asserts, this pessimistic view of the world is off the mark. "Reality" after all,

> is not inexorable or unchangeable. It happens to be this just as it could be something else. And if we so-called progressive thinkers want it to be something else, we have to struggle. (71)

Managing to be different — doing something different — is a struggle that is necessary if we want the academy "to be something else," something more than just an expression of the "immobilizing ideology of fatalism." In fact, it is vital, in every sense of the word, to recognize this ideology for what it is, and reject it. If we do not, we are doomed to fuel the continuation of inaction that allows what Parker calls "the divisive structures" that still dominate much of academia to remain fixed.[2]

To be willing to engage in this struggle requires the ability, as bell hooks exclaims, "to transgress." Like Freire, hooks views this ethical imperative, if you will, to transgress as a civic duty performed in the name of freedom. Also like Paulo Freire, bell hooks voices a position is in stark contrast to the ideology of fatalism. It is a position that is filled with a genuine sense of possibility and of hope. Even though the academy is a site of profound problems, bell hooks sees it as a place where political, social, and cultural transformation can happen. As she passionately argues in *Teaching to Transgress: Education as the Practice of Freedom*, the academy

> with all its limitations, remains a location of possibility. In that field of possibility we have the opportunity to labor for freedom, to demand of ourselves and our comrades, an openness of mind and heart that allows us to face reality even as we collectively imagine ways to move beyond boundaries, to transgress. This is education as the practice of freedom. (207)

We must work (labor, struggle) for a pedagogy of freedom. In turn, we must also begin working towards educational leadership as part of that pedagogy, as part of a critical practice. We must begin administrating as part of the liberating effort to enhance teaching and learning — that is, to enhance ethical democratic civic action in order to better the lives of those working and studying at schools, colleges, and universities, and for those (the vast majority of people) beyond the campus.

Sadly, we are experiencing a particularly difficult time in education. The situation is dire. In his introduction to the co-edited volume *Education as Enforcement: The Militarization and Corporatization of Schools*, Kenneth J. Saltman so accurately and powerfully summarizes the current state of things that I quote him here at length:

Education is becoming increasingly justified on the grounds of national security. This can be seen in the Hart-Rudman commission that in 2000 called for education to be classified as an issue of national security, in the increase of federal funding to school security simultaneous with cuts to community policing, in the continuation of the Troops to Teachers program, as well as the original *A Nation at Risk* report. Why is this? It is tied to the attack on social spending more generally, the antifederalist aspect of neoliberalism, a politics of containment rather than investment, the political efficacy of keeping large segments of the population uneducated and miseducated, the economic efficacy of keeping funds flowing to the defense and high-tech sectors and away from the segment of the population that are viewed as of little use to capital. As well, the working class, employed in low-skilled, low-paying service sector jobs, would be likely to complain or even organize if they were encouraged to question and think too much. Education and literacy are tied to political participation. Participation might mean that noncorporate elites would want social investment in public projects or at least projects that might benefit most people. That won't do. There is a reason that the federal government wants soldiers rather than say the glut of unemployed Ph.D.s in classrooms. Additionally, corporate globalization initiatives such as the FTAA seek to allow corporate competition into the public sector at an unprecedented level. In theory, public schools would have to compete with corporate for-profit schooling initiatives from any corporation in the world. By redefining public schooling as a national security issue, education could be exempted from the purview of this radical globalization that such agreements impose on other nations. Consistent with the trend, education for national security defines the public interest through the discourse of discipline that influences reforms that deskill teachers, inhibiting teaching as a critical and intellectual endeavor that aims to make a participatory citizenry capable of building the public sphere. (20)

Given this appraisal of the circumstance in which we live and work, it may not sound so melodramatic to suggest that pursuing

possibilities that undo the divisive structures of educational institutions — at any level of instruction or study — may be dangerous
work indeed. To engage in education as the practice of freedom
under these conditions is to risk being considered a threat to
national security. To challenge things, to dissent or resist, during
times of national crisis is to be subversive and unpatriotic.[3] All
efforts according to this logic must be focused on restoring and
maintaining law and order — so don't mess things up.

I say "mess things up" not to be glib or in any sense to trivialize
the importance of confronting those divisive structures that so
often immobilize us. Instead, I make use of that phrase because
of my own experience and those of colleagues who have been
accused of making a mess, of undermining the prevailing *doxa*
of a particular department or program or doing so on a larger
institutional scale. Attempting to implement strategies and practices that challenge, confront, and dismantle the long-standing
institutional habits and conventions of academia means breaking some things down, turning other things around (sometimes
on their head), and introducing new things and mixing stuff up
— that is, making a mess of "how the world is anyway."

For everyone already comfortably in place (and even for those
awkwardly and painfully placed) within the power grid, reconsidering and reevaluating the way the world is can mean trouble.
At best, such a rethinking means the hard work of honest self-
evaluation and assessment; at worst, such work can lead to expos-
ing oneself as hypocritically party to the ideology of fatalism. For
those cynical types that do populate academia, such an effort can
be pure theater; that is, it is all just a dog and pony show inspired
by political correctness. Such people are the bedrock of the ideology of fatalism.

While this dynamic is the case for just about every field and discipline, it is especially true for those of us involved with teacher education programs. Perhaps more so than any other discipline or professional field of study, teacher education is subject to the feckless nature of crude political jostling that occurs in cycles timed with elections. From voting for or against local school budgets to voicing affirmation or rejection of a country-wide referendum on national standards, teacher education is subject to the whim of, as Saltman declares, "the antifederalist aspect of neoliberalism."

The irony here is that these external forces claiming to demand reform and change are, much more often than not, little more than cynical tactics to further dismantle education as the practice of freedom. They have the paradoxical impact of supporting the "immobilizing ideology of fatalism" in the name of reforming education. Not surprisingly, educators and administrators hunker down dogmatically repeating their well-established mantra of perseverance: this too shall pass.

Because of the fights over what constitutes an appropriate curriculum or valid instrument of outcomes assessment, teacher educators are confronted by a bizarre choice: abandon what was done before or stubbornly dig in and find a way to remain the same. For schoolteachers and administrators, the result of this reductive binary option is stultification, even when things appear to change.

The schoolteachers and administrators I have worked with and spoken to about this issue have repeatedly and emphatically declared that it is their objective to remain the same (to whatever degree possible) during such times of innovation and reform. I cannot recall the number of teachers and administrators who, for example, simply paid lip service (rightly or wrongly) during the "whole language" movement and kept doing what they were *trained* to do.[4]

The fact that schoolteachers and administrators stick to their training is a problem and I am obviously critical of this tendency, this cognitive habit. But it is important to understand that I am not blaming them. (I know — big deal. How nice of me!) I make this potentially obnoxious distinction because, all too often, teachers and administrators alike are *only* blamed for this or that failure. They are, however, rarely engaged in a critical dialogue about their practice or theoretical foundations or perspective. (And by dialogue, I mean a mutually respectful exchange.)[5] So when merely confronted by change rather that authentically invited to be an agent of change, it is understandable — in fact reasonable, given the circumstances — that so many fall prey to "the immobilizing ideology of fatalism." How many times have you heard veteran teachers and administrators say, "Just wait two years or so, and we will be back to what we were doing ten years ago"? It is the now hackneyed chant of "waiting to go back to the future" that disheartened teachers and administrators whisper to and grunt at each other during staff development gatherings across the nation.

Those of us actively engaged in resisting fatalism and attempting, as bell hooks suggests, to transgress need to be cognizant of the restrictive binary dynamic that teachers and administrators experience. We must offer something different, something that encourages and fosters moving beyond the culture of fear and towards a community of hope. For those of you wondering (perhaps demanding to know) what that something is, I offer you again the insight and advice of Parker J. Palmer:

> The growth of craft depends on shared practice and honest
> dialogue among the people who do it. We grow by private trial
> and error, to be sure — but our willingness to try, and fail, as
> individuals is severely limited when we are not supported by a
> community that encourages such risks. When any function is
> privatized, the most likely outcome is that people will perform
> it conservatively, refusing to stray far from the silent consen-
> sus on what "works" — even when it clearly does not. (144)

That is to say, we must offer (build, reconstruct) communities
engaged in critical dialogue about what we do and how we do it.
Such communities can be established in teacher education programs willing to do more than train, programs that successfully
integrate scientific methodology, discipline-specific content, and
critical dialogue about the nature and dynamic of our unfinished
worlds.

Utopian and unpractical as it may sound at first, Palmer's strategy of establishing a "community that encourages such risks,"
such transgression, is, first and foremost, a concrete practical
plan. We must actually build, that is establish, the community
that will support our efforts to improve teaching and learning.
We must move beyond (transgress) the world that is, and com-
mit to engaging in exploring and declaring the world that is still
unfolding, the world that we are still unfolding. As Paulo Freire
puts it:

> Recognizing that precisely because we are constantly in the
> process of becoming and, therefore, are capable of observ-
> ing, comparing, evaluating, choosing, deciding, intervening,
> breaking with, and making options, we are ethical beings,
> capable of transgressing our ethical grounding. (92)

Because we can, we are obliged (ethically, not juridically) to work, struggle, and labor in the ongoing process of becoming who and what we are. This cannot happen if we merely train people to follow prefabricated lesson plans, prepare students for high-stakes tests, or ignore the social, historical, and cultural contexts in which we live and work. When we ignore or disregard Parker J. Palmer and Paulo Freire, as has been documented too many times, people wind up cheating, lying, and blaming anyone and everyone. Jonathan Kozol, for example, continues to provide documentation and testimony of what happens, and to whom, when we refuse to acknowledge the work that must be done.

Precisely because the stakes are professionally and intellectually high, we are from the start inculcated with the fear of messing up. Framing education within an increasingly corporate, competitive, and, as Saltman argues, militaristic model, puts us at odds with each other rather than encouraging us to work together to come up with strategies and alternatives that promote real cooperation and collaboration. This model has grown over the past few years, and has overtaken the very way we speak and think about education.

In his book *The Abandoned Generation: Democracy Beyond the Culture of Fear*, Henry A. Giroux persuasively details this shift in thinking:

> Within neoliberalism's market-driven discourse, corporate culture becomes both the model for the good life and the paradigmatic sphere for defining individual success and fulfillment. I use the term "corporate culture" to refer to an ensemble of ideological and institutional forces that functions politically and pedagogically to both govern organizational life through senior managerial control and to fashion compliant workers, depoliticized consumers, and passive citizens. Within the language and images of corporate culture,

citizenship is portrayed as an utterly solitary affair whose aim
is to produce competitive, self-interested individuals vying for
their own material and ideological gain. Corporate culture
largely cancels out or devalues social, class-specific, and racial
injustices of the existing social order by absorbing the democratic impulses and practices of civil society with the narrow
economic relations (for example, some neoliberal advocates
argue that the answer to states' staggering health care crises
is the sale of public assets, such as land, to private interests).
Corporate culture becomes an all-encompassing horizon for
producing market identities, values and practices. (158-159)

The emphasis on a neoliberal approach, generally, and its impact
on education specifically (namely the downsizing of resources
and the deskilling of teachers) has only intensified the ideology
of fatalism.

In a climate that perniciously promotes a rhetoric of greater
efficiency and accountability, messing around with a different
paradigm is greeted with suspicion and hostility, if it is acknowledged at all. Those who are managing to be different are doing
so at some real peril. Of course, such danger is not new. We can
cite Henry A. Giroux's struggle with Dr. John Silber, then-presi-
dent of Boston University, or a more recent battle over scholarship involving Cornel West, author of the bestseller *Race Matters*,
and Lawrence H. Summers, the embattled president of Harvard
University. (Giroux and West were offered options, but in essence
were pushed out.) But there have been and no doubt continue to
be casualties of being different who do not make the headlines or
even traverse the professional gossip highways of academia for a
host of reasons. In his excellent essay "Uncommon Differences:
On Political Correctness, Core Curriculum, and Democracy in
Education," in *I Won't Learn from You: And Other Thoughts on*

Creative Maladjustment, Herbert Kohl reminds us of the following institutional fact:

> The individual freedom to express unpopular or even new ideas in the classroom is controlled for both student and teacher by a system that marginalizes such behavior as deviant, disobedient, and "political." Even though there are occasional individual protests and even some successes, it is only when a protest becomes a collective and public matter that systemwide changes develop. (107)

Most individual efforts get thwarted by the divisive structures that consider "such behavior as deviant, disobedient and 'political.'" Unless we are fortunate enough to team up, managing to be different is typically an isolating, alienating, and frustrating struggle.

It would be simplistic and unfair to assume that everyone who is "different" is thoughtful, committed, intelligent, and generous; however, it is upsetting and unacceptable that everyone who is perceived as different is considered some sort of problem, unless that particular difference "works" for the institution. This may explain why schools, from high schools to prestigious universities, tolerate behavior that is considered deviant, disobedient, and, in some cases, even political, from the money-generating machinery known as college athletes and their coaches and athletic directors. From unethical "tutoring" and grade tampering to gambling and rape, schools and universities appear to have a much higher threshold for aberrant behavior (difference), when it is connected to large sums of money and school branding. Administrators tied to this are always quick to cite the now familiar justification provided by the ideology of fatalism: "But this is how the world is anyway."

Those of us dedicated to managing to be different will need to work together in solidarity with colleagues within our disciplines, in other departments and from other institutions (both educational and not). But as Parker J. Palmer tells us,

> Community does not emerge spontaneously from some relational reflex, especially not in the complex and often conflicted institutions where most [of us] work. If we are to have communities of discourse about teaching and learning — communities that are intentional about the topics to be pursued and the ground rules to be practiced — we need leaders who can call people toward that vision. (156)

That is, we need leaders, and must become leaders, who call people toward a vision of possibility and hope. We must demand, and become, leaders that will expand and extend the myopic perspective engendered and maintained by the ideology of fatalism, an ideology that ultimately blinds us to "that vision" and leaves us scrambling through a desperate darkness of despair, indifference, and fear.

3

IT ONLY LOOKS LIKE A MESS

I remember sitting at a large seminar table with a group of New York City high school teachers. We were finishing up a wide-ranging discussion about the requirements, content, and teaching strategies for a special course for high school seniors that was grant funded. It was a college class, not an advanced placement high school course. In addition to other educational innovations that were part of the overall grant, funding was provided to include this team-taught course: one college faculty member would be paired with a high school teacher. Among my other job obligations and duties at the time, I was the administrator responsible for finding interested and qualified college instructors from the social science and humanities divisions. I was the liaison who introduced the professors to their high school teaching partners. I also hosted gatherings that would allow everyone to get to know each other and work out professional and pedagogical issues as well as fine-tune the course.

At this particular meeting, only high school teachers were present. (Some meetings were exclusively for the high school teachers, some just for the college instructors, and others included representatives of all the participants.) Although most of the team pairings worked very well, there were, occasionally, significant problems. One recurring issue was the "professor versus teacher" dynamic. There were many different manifestations of this interaction, some subtle and difficult to identify at first, others as blatant as they were outrageously petty. At this meeting we were discussing the tendency of some high school teachers to defer to the professor, "the expert," even though they disagreed with something the professor said, or had an alternative position on some matter that they wanted the students to consider. In some cases, these teachers remained silent despite the fact that there had been an erroneous statement made by the professor. We had just finished critically interrogating ourselves about some of the professional and personal reasons — the social, cultural, and political reasons — why such a dynamic might exist at all, and had agreed to meet the following week to continue our dialogue.

Some of the teachers were standing, some were stretching, and others were getting more coffee. The seminar table was strewn with the remains of half-eaten bagels, empty donut boxes, the still sought-after crumbs of homemade zucchini bread, baked by one of the teachers, and some juice containers and coffee cups. There was something festive looking about the whole scene, and one could sense an atmosphere of collegial solidarity and togetherness. Collectively we exuded a confidence and an air of satisfaction regarding our good work that morning. There was the kind of buzz in the room that typically follows productive gatherings. Teachers voiced their opinions, offered analysis and interpretation of their experiences, and felt real progress was made concerning a number of important issues. The meeting was over and people were just talking to each other, one to one and in various small groups. The mood was upbeat and hopeful.

Suddenly, it was gone; a nervous quietness fell over the room. I had not noticed, but just as we were breaking up, the principal of the high school had appeared. Like a specter, his presence frightened the teachers. He stood dead still, staring sternly into the silenced room that just moments ago had been filled with an animated hum. Before completely entering the room he spoke: "What's this mess? I thought this was a seminar room; was there a party that I wasn't invited to?" I hesitated, wondering whether or not someone else might speak up, but instinctively replied, "It only looks like a mess." He turned towards me and countered sarcastically, "I know, there's something I'm not seeing, right?" Again I hesitated but this time not because I was waiting (hoping) for someone else to speak first. I delayed because I wanted to choose my words carefully — we had had this back and forth before. Finally, I spoke: "Actually, there's a lot you do not see." I then paused, but for just the shortest moment. I quickly finished my comment, "For example, there's another loaf of zucchini bread, would you like some?" He stoically endured my sentences and, to his credit, he readily accepted a slice of the bread. But the damage was done; the mood had dramatically shifted. "His" teachers were already cleaning up the mess: order was being restored.

As the principal paced the room, the teachers were saying their goodbyes and heading back to the high school. He nodded at some with approval and said a quick word as they left. When all the teachers were gone he turned and cautioned me, "Be careful about messing things up." He offered this warning not so much as a threat as much as a bit of "practical wisdom" gained from years of surviving the system. "If you keep having these discussions, these 'dialogues' as you like to call them, *my* teachers are going to get the wrong idea, and you will undermine my authority." He continued, "This might work well for you and your college colleagues, although I doubt it, but things work differently at the high school level. The governance of the school is my responsibility." He looked around the emptied room, and seemed to be finished but added, as if it were an afterthought, "Besides, it's not like you're really going to listen to them and be able to change things. You'll only disappoint and frustrate them."

Paternalistically — somehow disapproving and patronizing at the same time — he concluded with a sigh, "You'll only make a mess of things. They really can't handle this sort of indulgence. You'll see. It will all blow up, and I'll have to clean up the mess." His tone was somber and full of resignation. I was being given much more than a simple heads-up. I was subjected to a disputation, an emotional expostulation, by a true believer of his faith. But I could see that he was weary and grew impatient with his own oration — he no doubt had recited this argument many times before. By rote, it seemed, he explained how the world really works and why there was little, if anything, I could do about it, other than mess things up.

As he spoke I could feel the muted annoyance of his words; they clung to me like an unbearable humidity, making me lethargic and dazed. I wanted to interrupt him and stop him from making me sweat. (As with many administrators of his ilk, making people sweat was part of his job description.) I wanted to prevent him from extinguishing the possibilities ignited that morning.

But I remained silent. I knew at that moment I was hearing not just his voice, but the voice of all who speak from within an ideology of fatalism. His narrative was far more difficult to bear than the run of the mill reprimand. He was elaborating a worldview in which no one could expect, much less initiate, change; no one, according to him, was ultimately up to the task. He was stating his renunciation of hope and offered me decades of history as evidence to silence any talk of other worlds. The seminar room suddenly felt tight, claustrophobic; I was being held prisoner by a guardian of "how the world is."

I was hearing the voice of Dostoevski's Grand Inquisitor:

> But Thou didst think too highly of men therein, for they are slaves, of course, though rebellious by nature. Look round and judge; fifteen centuries have passed; look upon them. Whom hast Thou raised up to Thyself? I swear, man is weaker and baser by nature than Thou hast believed him! Can he, can he do what Thou didst? By showing him so much respect, Thou didst, as it were, cease to feel for him, for Thou didst ask far too much from him — Thou who hast loved him more than Thyself! Respecting him less, Thou wouldst have asked less of him. That would have been more like love, for his burden would have been lighter. He is weak and vile. What though he is everywhere now rebelling against our power, and proud of his rebellion? It is the pride of a child and a schoolboy. They are little children rioting and barring out the teacher at school. But their childish delight will end; it will cost them dear. (34-35)

I was the one now sighing. He self-righteously concluded and left me to mourn the loss of my naiveté. But I wasn't mourning and I had long ago stopped being naïve; I was, however, lamenting the struggles that lay ahead. In the solitude of the once vibrant room, I meandered through the spaces and openings created earlier that morning. Proudly, somewhat defiantly, I reclaimed the hope and possibilities of a different world, a world whose existence I never doubted, a world full of people, as bell hooks describes, transgressing the boundaries that have traditionally limited our imaginations and restricted our actions.

I was attempting to build a community of interlocutors that seriously, honestly, and authentically questioned and challenged one another about their teaching practice and beyond. This group included everyone I came in contact with: college administrators and faculty and schoolteachers and their administrators. As an educator committed to being critically engaged with teaching I came to expect such dialogue; as an administrator, I was in a position to invite others to come join the dialogue and support each other. Genuine conversation about teaching makes a difference, and our weekly gathering was just one of the ways in which I was trying to create and sustain the dialogue. As Parker J. Palmer notes:

> Good talk about good teaching can take many forms and involve many conversation partners — and it can transform teaching and learning. But it will happen only if leaders expect it, invite it, and provide hospitable space for the conversation to occur. (160)

I knew that in order to make a difference, I needed consciously to pursue this kind of educational leadership. I wanted to be the sort of leader who was willing to invite and coordinate, to welcome and support, to have an agenda and let things go where they needed to, a leader who was willing to risk making a mess. Palmer tells us:

Becoming a leader of that sort — one who opens, rather than occupies, space — requires the same inner journey we have been exploring for teachers. It is a journey beyond fear and into authentic selfhood, a journey toward respecting otherness and understanding how connected and resourceful we all are. As those inner qualities deepen, the leader becomes better able to open spaces in which people feel invited to create communities of mutual support. (161)

As disingenuous as it may sound to some, I had committed to making such a journey, and was looking for others to move beyond the fear with me. When colleagues, teachers, and administrators alike are respected, and they are able to sense it; a space does open and dialogue begins. It begins naturally because of the work itself and the people who do it. They want to tell their stories, and are willing, even eager, to listen to others when they believe that the interactions are authentic and mutually respectful. And as Palmer suggests, there are many different venues for this dialogue to unfold.

Sandra Jackson and Jose Solis Jordan offer us a moving and encouraging example of another way to initiate and sustain the dialogue. In the introduction to their co-edited volume, *I've got a story to tell*, they note the need for and difficulty of establishing dialogue, specifically for educators of color.

Because of the barriers confronting scholars and professors of color in higher education, it is not uncommon for us to articulate that in a real sense we have learned how not to talk (about issues of race, sexuality, and gender) because of the fiercely political, social, and cultural environment of the academy, which impinges upon one's experiences in relationship to one's peers, students, as well as administrators regarding not only the curriculum but also pedagogy, scholarship, promotion, tenure — indeed one's very existence there. [...] This makes the possibility of "honest dialogue" problematic; hence, the commensurability of differences vis-à-vis dialogical exercises remains as perplexing as ever. Yet assuming that one arrives at a point where dialogue can take place, assuming such is possible, the question of respect and trust must be addressed. (3)

Their book, *I've got a story to tell,* simultaneously offers the reader testimony regarding the difficulty of establishing genuine dialogue and an example of successfully having such dialogue. In this case, their book becomes a means of initiating and sustaining meaningful dialogue concerning the experiences of people of color in academia, and in doing so directly addresses issues that matter to everyone in academia. Their book itself is an example of a way that leadership can create openings and spaces for educators to speak. The stories that have to be told are the stories that would not get told if Jackson and Jordan did not, as Parker J. Palmer asserts, "provide hospitable space for the conversation to occur," in this case, that space is a volume in which contributors can tell their stories.

In the process of producing their book, Jackson and Jordan also provide an opportunity for their contributors to publish, which in turn helps these thoughtful and critical educators to remain part of the conversation professionally. Given the pressures of publishing, this book gives the contributors the chance to write about important topics, issues and themes and gain professional legitimacy in the act of doing so. This particular way of providing a hospitable space allows for dialogue between contributors and their readers; dialogue among the contributors themselves; and dialogue among publishers, writers, and their audience. This is important because, in higher education, the dialogue is often silenced, in part because there are not enough academically acceptable "spaces" in which to have one. By providing educators and scholars publishing opportunities we help create communities engaged in sustained discussion about what it is we do, something that increasingly gets ignored or devalued in this era of commercialization and corporatization of education at every level of instruction.[1]

With the government's growing interests in using a business model to improve the quality of education nationwide, schools and universities are, at an ever-increasing frequency, viewing education as a product to be efficiently marketed to students (the consumers). Educators become entrepreneurs, competing for a greater market share. What is particularly disturbing, from the perspective of attempting to establish communities in which dialogue can flourish, is the fact that the corporate model has no inherent interest in or need for a dialogue about hope — that is to say, an ethical and meaningful vision of the world, of the future per se. Such a model diminishes the real value of teaching and learning in the process of commodifying them, making them the "privileged goods" to be bought and sold. What gets tossed out in the manufacturing of a "trained" workforce is any notion of education as vital to freedom, to democracy, and to a citizenry capable of engaging in public debate about such things.

In *The Abandoned Generation: Democracy beyond the Culture of Fear*, Henry A. Giroux argues the following:

> In the corporate model, knowledge is privileged as a form of investment in the economy, but appears to have little value in terms of self-definition, social responsibility, or the capacities of individuals to expand the scope of freedom, justice, and democracy. Stripped of ethical and political considerations, knowledge offers limited, if any, insights into how schools should educate students to push against the oppressive

boundaries of gender, class, race and age discrimination. Nor does such a corporate language provide the pedagogical conditions for students to critically engage school knowledge as an ideology deeply implicated in issues and struggles concerning the production of identities, culture, power and history. Education is a moral and political practice, and always presupposes an introduction to and preparation for particular forms of social life, a particular rendering of what community is, and an idea of what the future might hold. (173)

In the corporate model, notions of freedom and democracy are replaced by access, market share, and profit margin. Education becomes little more than a mechanism through which individuals are reconfigured (reproduced, if you will) from humans — social agents — in search of meaning into consuming subjects seeking something to buy and own.[2] More and more people struggle with this self-alienating mode of social interaction. They are doing so, as Giroux notes, precisely at a time when education is abandoning its once critical role in the development of the moral and social character of individuals "to expand the scope of freedom, justice and democracy."

Despite all of the hyper-charged rhetoric coming from social conservatives and the religious right that suggests the opposite, education is being re-formed, to use that much abused word — unfortunately, it is being sculpted into the image of corporate America. It is being transformed from a "hospitable space" to conduct critical inquiry and debate into a place that meets the needs of employers. "The message here," Giroux tells us,

is clear. Knowledge with a high market value is what counts, while those fields, such as the liberal arts and humanities, that cannot be quantified in such terms will either be under-funded or allowed to become largely irrelevant in the hierarchy of academic knowledge. (175)

Whatever else education might be, it does little good — from a corporate perspective — if it engenders individuals who might question the ethics of globalization. It becomes increasingly important not to mess things up by having educators getting together to discuss teaching and learning, especially if such dialogue pushes for a different model of education, indeed a different model of the world.

It may strike some as bold, but why should educators sit idly by without attempting to rethink schooling, and why should administrators, educational leaders, not expect such dialogue or invite it to happen? In the name of pragmatism, many in education have opted not to be different, have accepted, like the principal of the high school, "the world as it is" — that is, have accepted reality. Therefore, they cannot help but see efforts to be different as fantasy, as "troubling," leading to disappointments and worse: the nullification of the world as it is now known through the pragmatic discourse of neoliberalism. In his *Pedagogy of Hope*, Paulo Freire puts it this way: "We are surrounded by a pragmatic discourse that would have us adapt to the facts of reality. Dreams, and utopia, are called not only useless, but positively impeding" (7). We are encompassed by those who participate in the maintenance of fatalism in the name of being realistic. Sadly, this form of realism leads to nihilism and a pedagogy of hopelessness.

I have too often witnessed firsthand and have been told too many times by educators and administrators that trying to do things differently only leads to problems, only "makes a mess." After a while, one becomes unwilling even to bother, because the consequences can be quite severe. In an effort to survive, everyone attempts, as Freire tells us, to "adapt to the facts of reality." Elsewhere, in his book *Education for Critical Consciousness*, Freire points out: "If man is incapable of changing reality, he adjusts himself instead. Adaptation is behavior characteristic of the animal sphere; exhibited by man, it is symptomatic of his dehumanization" (4). Without hope, we opt for a mode of survival that only perpetuates the very structure and practices that make change threatening and difficult, and erodes the possibilities that democratic efforts can bring about. We become subject to despair and paranoia; the future is bleak and we cannot trust anyone. The world makes sense, but only to the degree that it delineates and restricts authentic human interaction. The boundaries produced by the ideology of fatalism get put back in place and are reinforced.

In isolation and conforming to the facts of a corporate reality, educators and administrators alike find themselves laboring in what appears to be a futile effort to improve their "product." Interestingly, it seems that the more they actually do produce (for example, more research, grants, articles, books, but especially better test scores), the more pressure there is from outside the schooling system to produce an even better product. This makes those within the schooling system, who accept and adapt to the "facts of reality," party to their own commodification and alienation.

As gauche as it may be these days, one cannot help but think here of Karl Marx's unfinished essay "Estranged Labor," published in the collection, *The Economic and Philosophic Manuscripts of 1844*:

> The worker becomes all the poorer the more wealth he produces, the more his production increases in power and size. The worker becomes an ever cheaper commodity the more

commodities he creates. With the increasing value of the world of things proceeds in direct proportion the devaluation of the world of men. Labor produces not only commodities: it produces itself and the worker as a commodity — and this in the same general proportion in which it produces commodities. (107)

Not like workers, but *as* workers, educators and administrators are directly involved in their own demise. In his concluding chapter from *The Abandoned Generation*, Giroux elaborates:

There is more at work here than despair; there are the harsh lessons of financial deprivation, overburdened work loads, and powerlessness. As power shifts away from the faculty to the managerial sectors of the university, adjunct faculty increase in number while effectively being removed from the faculty governance process. In short, the hiring of part-time faculty to minimize costs simultaneously maximizes managerial control over faculty and the educational process itself. As their ranks are depleted full-time faculty live under the constant threat of being either given heavier work loads or of simply having their tenure contracts eliminated or drastically redefined through "post-tenure reviews." These structural and ideological factors send a chill through higher education faculty and undermine the collective power faculty need to challenge the increasing corporate-based, top-down administrative structures that are becoming commonplace in many colleges and universities. (177)

Managing to be different in this context means engaging with everyone committed to refusing to adapt to the "facts of reality." And there are ways to resist, ways of being different. But it does take working together, creating opportunities for dialogue and building solidarity. From meeting with colleagues to supporting collective representation (yes, unions), there are ways and means of countering the impact of the corporate imperative. This means that educators must demand (fight for) positions of responsibility and power, and be willing to view educational leadership as a critical practice, in and out of the classroom — namely, in the administrative functions of their schools and colleges. Simply becoming a chair or a dean doesn't guarantee that change will automatically happen. Any effort, any challenge, will demand a willingness, and skilled ability, to break from the ideology of fatalism and struggle beyond the boundaries that keep us neatly in place. This means being critically engaged with the power dynamics of the institution and willing to take risks. We must risk supporting veteran educators as well as colleagues just out of graduate school; we must expect and create "hospitable space" for dialogue, because in talking together we are given the opportunity to know each other and gain mutual respect. And with that respect, we can begin to demand integrity throughout educational institutions and not simply pay lip service to "quality control." We must find ways of disrupting the "divisive structures," as Parker J. Palmer has called them, and mix things up.[3] In doing so, we must be prepared for the fallout, the flack, and the outrage over destroying the world as it is known. But remember, in time everyone committed to teaching and learning, to social justice and freedom, will come to see that "it only looks like a mess."

4

POWER GAMES:
AUGUSTO BOAL AND THE
POSITIONING OF POWER

In the previous chapters I have discussed some of the ways in which power circulates and works its way through educational institutions. Sometimes we can see the effects as things unfold; sometimes the impact is felt or noticed only later on. Power can take different forms of expression — for example, tenure and promotion reviews, appointments to be chair or dean, salaries, workload, schedules, and so on. But power can also make itself known through attitudes, values, and positions. We have already seen how "the ideology of fatalism" and "the corporate model" have had an impact on education — that is, on students, faculty, and the culture of academia. Our encounters and struggles with power occur every day, yet, in many ways, it remains the word unspoken. We might say or hear, "How did Norm get away with that," or "Did you hear what they did to Lizzette," but rarely is there explicit and useful dialogue about how power works. We discuss neither our attitudes towards it nor what we can do when it is working against good teaching and learning — against what it is that we stand for in education.

Perhaps part of the problem, as we already noted in Chapter Two, is "the culture of fear" that is pervasive throughout educational institutions. Because we so often do lack power we attempt to stay clear of situations that we believe can cause us unwanted attention or problems. Sometimes (more often than many of us would like to admit), we act as if we are only spectators of events and decisions taking place all around us and refuse to see ourselves as participants, even when there are opportunities to act and be fully engaged. We believe that we can position ourselves at a safe distance from power; in other words, we think we can hide. (As I mentioned in Chapter One, hiding is at best a very temporary measure.)

We actively work at ignoring and distorting where we stand in relationship to power because, as Freire and Palmer have argued, we either surrender to the way things are — accepting our fate — or we are frightened by it all. As a result, many people never question where they actually stand in relation to power: they say to themselves, "Why bother, given how things are," or are simply afraid to ask — if you speak up it will cost you. But anyone genuinely interested in the issue of educational leadership must be prepared to inquire into the nature of power and be willing and able to discuss it with colleagues. By abdicating our responsibilities, we only play into the hands of those who would manipulate things, those who use power unjustly and ultimately do harm to our colleagues, our students, and ourselves. At some point we must ask ourselves, where do we stand?

The Brazilian theater director and theorist Augusto Boal, in his engaging book, *Games for Actors and Non-Actors*, tells us,

> The word "theater" is so rich in different meanings, some complementary, some contradictory, that we never know what we mean when we talk about theater. Which theater do we mean? (XXV)

This is so because theater can refer to a place, the theater. It can be a building, an outdoor stage, and so on. Theater can also mean the inauguration of a president, the funeral of a pope, or a parade; as Boal notes, "[t]he word 'rite' can be used to designate these manifestations of theater" (XXV). But theater, he goes on to say,

> can also be the repetitive acts of daily life. We perform the play of breakfast, the scene of going to work, the act of working, the epilogue of supper, the epic of Sunday lunch with the family, etc.; like actors in a long run of a successful show, repeating the same lines to the same partner, executing the same movements, at the same times, thousands of times over. Life can become a series of mechanisations, as rigid and as lifeless as the movements of a machine. (XXV)

I have quoted this passage before, in Teaching Values, where my theme was the performative nature of teaching and being in the world. I use it again here to emphasize the performative aspect of our daily academic life (ritual): the "theater," if you will, of committee meetings, department meetings, official gatherings, private conversations with colleagues and with students and their parents, conversations with administrators, etc. We are actively performing our roles within the power grid, the often "divisive structures," as Palmer calls them, and I want to use Boal as a means for looking at ourselves in this context.

Concluding the preface to his book, Boal suggests that theater is "the art of looking at ourselves" (XXX). In order to get actors and non-actors to better look at themselves, Boal offers us "games" to perform. I want to talk specifically about one game, "the great game of power."[1] The game is simple: all you need is a space (typically a room, but this could happen outdoors), a table, six chairs, and a bottle.

> First of all, participants are asked to come up one at a time and arrange the objects so as to make one chair become the most powerful object, in relation to the other chairs, the table and the bottle. Any of the objects can be moved or placed on top of each other, or on their sides, or whatever, but none of the objects can be removed altogether from the space. The group will run through a great number of variations of the arrangement. (150)

There is another phase of the game that I will talk about below, but for the moment I want to focus on this first activity.

I have used this game in a number of settings — including a seminar for senior administrators at a prestigious hospital, an annual professional development gathering for teachers, a group of high-school students doing a project on building community, and a class exercise for a graduate course on cross-cultural communications, among other venues. In each setting the participants were hesitant to perform the task. They all seem confused, at first, by the prospect of empowering an inanimate object, especially a chair. But eventually, someone is willing to risk looking foolish. They either feel foolish in the sense that they are somewhat embarrassed to be the first to try to arrange a bottle, table, and chair while others look on skeptically, or they worry that they will not be able to accomplish the task and publicly fail at something, even an innocuous game. By the way, I never introduce the game as the great game of power, but only as an exercise or activity to help look at how we see power.

Although he does not instruct us to do so in his book, I add to the instructions given by Boal. Each time participants arrange things to their satisfaction, I ask them to tell the rest of the group why it is that the arrangement works for them. I then ask the group if they "see" it as well. Sometimes they do; sometimes they do not. It doesn't really matter. If they do see it, I'll ask for a bit more of an elaboration, suggesting that I sort of see it, but could use a bit more help. If the group does not see it, I ask them why not and could they explain why they don't see it — what other chair, if not the one so identified, has the power? In either case, discussion unfolds quickly. People offer elaborate interpretations and justifications for why they do or do not see things according to the way someone has arranged the world.

After a number of positionings and repositionings, people are into the game and actively attempt to take the current arrangement of power and disrupt it by envisioning an alternative configuration. Even though participants offer their rationales and defenses for their arrangements, they still see themselves as manipulating inanimate objects and are relaxed about swiping power from a colleague; after all, it is just a game. When it appears that we have finished with this exercise and we, as a group, agree that one particular arrangement works well, and we all can "see" it, I introduce the second phase.

Augusto Boal tells us:

> Then, when a suitable arrangement has been arrived at, an arrangement which the group feels is the most powerful, a participant is asked to enter the space and take up the most powerful position, without moving anything. Once someone is in place, the other members of the group can enter the space and try to place themselves in an even more powerful position, and take away the power the first person established. (150)

Typically, there is a return of the hesitancy to go first. Despite the fact that the group has been engaged and animated by the first phase of the activity, there is some anxiety about placing oneself into the mix. This is especially the case when there are participants with varying degrees of power from an organization or institution playing at the same time — for example, a principal and the staff of a school, the vice president for nursing and the nursing directors of the various departments, and so on. But as is the case with the first phase of the game, someone volunteers to go.

This time around, I don't ask for an explanation from the first person who enters the space; everyone understands that this person "sees" herself or himself as successfully plugged into the power grid, and awaits a challenge, a usurpation of power. Unlike the first phase of the game, the participants can no longer move things around; they cannot rearrange the bottle, table, or chairs; these things are now fixed. The world with its power structure is there waiting for them. All they can do is place themselves somewhere in the already-arranged space of power. They do have the choice of placing themselves here, there, or anywhere within the existing space, but once placed, they are subject to the "power moves" of those who enter the power grid after them.

It is possible, in principle, that the person who gets to choose first, who gets to place her or himself before others, will do so perfectly and prevent any subsequent move to offset or disrupt her or his position of power. This is, however, very unlikely for many reasons — even a master chess player needs to move more than once. And unlike chess, those who move after the fact, perform without Cartesian precision; there are elements that enter into the power space that are emotional and psychological. In other words, power can shift sometimes even if one could make a valid argument that it really should not have changed. Like a bad call in sports, sometimes what ought to be the case turns out not to be the case.

The participants who enter the space after the first person are asked to explain or justify why they believe they have taken power away from the first participant; it is up to the remaining players to decide. If they think that the original participant remains in the position of power, they will usually ignore the challenger (almost to a person) and place themselves somewhere within the space in response to the first participant. Whatever choice is made here will need to be justified. Actually, if everyone agrees that a certain move is successful, there is no need to defend one's position because that new position is now considered the one to challenge. But I will then ask them to explain to me why this move has been successful.

One of the many interesting things that happens is that the explanations and justifications offered are very often unconscious worldviews. The participants are into the game (some get noticeably competitive) and are unaware that they say some quite interesting things in their attempts to fix or take power. For example, someone who arranged the chairs in a particular order might say, "This chair has power because it looks out onto the other chairs.

It looks and it is judging them." But someone else might see that same arrangement and say, "Hold on a second. Given the way you have set things up, it looks to me as if your chair is the one being looked at and judged, kind of the way a group of judges looks at a contestant or a jury looks at a defendant." It gets more revealing when the participants insert themselves into the space of power.

There was one time when someone stated that because the previous participant was a woman, she still did not take power from the person before her (a male participant). At least it did not look that way to her. In response to this, the next participant (also a woman) placed herself next to the other female facing the man. The explanation that followed included the rationale that now there were two women staring down the man. When another participant, another woman, said, "I don't see it," there was an uproar from the other women participating in the game. Still more interesting was when the woman who said she didn't get it went on to say, "Besides, the rules state that each individual was to take power, not build teams of those who shared power." The next person to go, another woman, placed herself across from the two women and the man, claiming that she now had the power because see was looking at everyone having a power struggle but was outside the fight.

Another person took this position another step and placed himself at the fringe of the designated space. The room we were using at the time was empty save for the six chairs, the bottle, the table, and the participants. This person decided that by placing himself far away from the power struggle (the center) he would in fact claim power from the outside (the margin). Of course, people quickly challenged him about retreating to the margins; they wondered about the legitimacy and plausibility of claiming power from beyond the center. It led to a very interesting and revealing dialogue about moving to the margin, away from the center of things, in order to empower oneself. Participants considered what such a move might entail politically and ethically. That discussion quickly turned into a useful dialogue among white participants and those of color about where power resides in the United States generally and how self-marginalization can be viewed (by some) as an act of resistance, of protest, and therefore as an expression of power.

It was argued that transgressing the normative space and the understood limit of power (or at least attempting to do so) represents an effort to establish autonomy — in this case, sovereignty. The act of transgression, of self-marginalization, is understood as an act of agency and thus an expression of power. In the act of crossing the line, the previously established limit (of the domain of power), the participant announces his distance, his power — I am here and decidedly not there! But in the act of calling attention to himself through his leaving (his absence from the center), he simultaneously renders his act of leaving somewhat null and void. In the subversive act of transgression, of turning his back on the power at the center of things, he makes his absence known; and in revealing his agency, his power, he also identifies it, and names it. This, however, puts him at risk: the very act of transgression gets negated, if not erased, in the calling of it to attention. The power that was expressed in the act of transgressing was private; but it is private no longer and is now made public. With the publicity comes the far reach of the strong arm of the center; the margin is defined by it.

In the collection of essays and interviews titled *Language, Counter-Memory, Practice*, the French philosopher Michel Foucault points out that transgression

> is not related to the limit as black to white, the prohibited to the lawful, the outside to the inside, or as the open area of a building to its enclosed spaces. Rather, their relationship takes the form of a spiral which no simple infraction can exhaust. Perhaps it is like a flash of lightning in the night which, from the beginning of time, gives a dense and black intensity to the night it denies, which lights up the night from the inside, from top to bottom, and yet owes to the dark the stark clarity of its manifestation, its harrowing and poised singularity; the flash loses itself in this space it marks with its sovereignty and becomes silent now that it has given a name to obscurity. (35)

In our case, by stepping out, into the place where one assumes power cannot reach, we have, in fact, extended the reach of (institutional) power. The great game of power had given us a chance to experience, analyze, and discuss some important dimensions of power.

What proved especially useful to the group of participants described above was linking their experiences with the great game of power to their teaching and learning experiences. These participants were teachers and many made the connections right away and introduced variations on what we were witnessing in the game from their school experiences. One teacher made reference to Herbert Kohl's excellent essay, "I won't learn from you," from his book with the same title. In it, Kohl tell us:

> Learning how to not-learn is an intellectual and social challenge; sometimes you have to work very hard at it. It consists of an active, often ingenious, willful rejection of even the most compassionate and well-designed teaching. It subverts

attempts at remediation as much as it rejects learning in the first place. It was through insight into my own not-learning that I began to understand the inner world of students who chose to not-learn what I wanted to teach. Over the years I've come to side with them in their refusal to be molded by a hostile society and have come to look upon not-learning as positive and healthy in many situations. (2)

The teacher who mentioned Kohl's essay said that his experience in the great game of power allowed him to appreciate the full richness of Kohl's position, which the teacher had previously considered well-meaning but a bit too liberal. Others from the group began making similar claims and related their experience with students, colleagues, and administrators.

"Not-learning" as a conscious choice, understood as an act of defiance and resistance, is certainly still difficult (and exhausting) to deal with, but it is an expression of agency and power, a willful rejection of "world as it is," and not merely a result of failure to learn. As Kohl puts it:

> Not-learning and unlearning are both central techniques that support changes of consciousness and help people develop positive ways of thinking and speaking in opposition to dominant forms of oppression. Not-learning in particular requires a strong will and ability to take the kinds of pressure exerted by people whose power you choose to question. (23)

Kohl rightly notes the agency in the act of "not-learning" and in the expression of choosing to question authority and power. This doesn't mean that the student will succeed in achieving an identity that is without damage, conflict, or contradiction. But the teachers participating in the great game of power began to see that their pedagogical strategies had to address power itself in ways they had not fully considered: they acknowledged the need to interrogate that look of resistance as something more than the mere "attitude" of an uncooperative student. They began to see that, as educators, they were obligated to reconsider their positions — ethically, culturally, and politically.

In her essay "The Oppositional Gaze," from her book *Black Looks: Race and Representation*, bell hooks further expands Kohl's analysis when she argues the following:

> Spaces of agency exist for black people, wherein we can both interrogate the gaze of the Other but also look back, and at one another, naming what we see. The "gaze" has been and is a site of resistance for colonized black people globally. Subordinates in relations of power learn experientially that there is a critical gaze, one that "looks" to document, one that is oppositional. In resistance struggle, the power of the dominated to assert agency by claiming and cultivating "awareness" politicizes "looking" relations — one learns to look a certain way in order to resist. (116)

One positions oneself and one gazes back at power: one looks a certain way. Children do it, women contesting patriarchy do it, prisoners do it; everyone who stands in opposition to the status quo does it or surrenders.

The usefulness and applicability of the great game of power to educational leadership, I hope, are equally clear. One example that comes readily to mind is that of the power dynamic I have witnessed more than once in my career: the hurt and angry junior faculty member who becomes a self-fulfilling prophecy regarding tenure. There are many different versions of this narrative, but they all seem to contain the following element: a junior faculty member who comes to view her or himself (often accurately) as having been somehow wronged or underappreciated and needs to reestablish her or his sense of self-worth by actively (publicly) confronting, resisting, and transgressing the limits of power oppressing her or him. The endgame is set in motion. For those who have witnessed it (or have suffered from it, or have perpetrated it, or have intervened to stop it, etc.), you do not need me to retell this too frequent academic drama, and for those of you who have not, I think you can imagine the various possible plot lines and outcomes (all of them are messy and most of them are unacceptable). The issue that I want to emphasize here is that all too often the great game of power gets played — except it is for real — and those playing it (on both sides) too often do not understand that there are other possibilities, other ways to play and finish the game. But in order for this to happen, all the players would have to come to terms with how power works in educational institutions.

In *Homo Academicus*, his book about the power structure of French academia, Pierre Bourdieu points out the harsh reality of the game.

> Like all forms of loosely institutionalized power which may not be delegated to representatives, strictly academic power can only be accumulated and maintained at the cost of constant and heavy expenditure of time. The result is, as Weber has already noted, that the acquisition and exercise of administrative power in the university field — that of dean or recteur [vice-chancellor], for example — or the unofficial power of an elector to professorships or an influential member of an electoral college, or of commissions and committees of all kinds, tends in fact to compromise the accumulation of a capital of scientific authority and vice versa. Like the accumulation of symbolic capital in a pre-capitalist society, where the objectification of economic and cultural mechanisms is not very advanced, the accumulation of a specific capital of academic authority demands payment in kind, that is, with one's own

> time, in order to control the network of institutions where aca-
> demic power is accumulated and exercised and also to enter
> into the exchanges of which these gatherings are the occasion
> and where a capital of services rendered is gradually consti-
> tuted, which is indispensable to the establishment of complici-
> ties, alliances and clienteles. (95-96)

In other words, it costs, in every sense of the word. Sadly, many individuals pay too high a price. But if we are to claim a stake in the game, specifically as leaders — that is, claim agency and therefore responsibility — we must acknowledge the full force of the dynamic of power in all of its vicissitudes.

This does not mean that in order to succeed in academia one must sell out or become complicit with those who are unfair or impose the corporate model. But it does mean that there is a necessary (institutionally established) power dynamic that must be acknowledged, navigated, and negotiated. Even if one stands in opposition to the dominant power bloc, one is doing so in the space of educational power and, therefore, must be prepared to take (and advocate) a stand. As Giroux puts it in *The Abandoned Generation*,

> Challenging the encroachment of corporate power is essential
> if democracy is to remain a defining principle of education
> and everyday life. Educators, students, and others must create
> organizations capable of mobilizing civic dialogue, provide an
> alternative conception of the meaning and purpose of higher
> education, and develop political organizations that can influ-
> ence legislation to challenge corporate power's ascendancy
> over the institutions and mechanisms of civil society. In stra-
> tegic terms, revitalizing public dialogue suggests that faculty,
> students and administrators need to take seriously the impor-
> tance of defending higher education as an institution of civic
> culture whose purpose is to educate students for active and
> critical citizenship. To do so educators, students, and others
> will have to provide the rationale and mobilize efforts toward

creating enclaves of resistance, new public spaces to counter
official forms of public pedagogy, and institutional spaces
that highlight, nourish, and evaluate the tension between civil
society and corporate power, while simultaneously struggling
to prioritize citizen rights over consumer rights. (188-189)

"Challenging" can take many forms. It can take place in the
creation of programs and courses of study that enhance critical
thinking for students and educators, in the establishment of professional development programs and support for junior faculty,
and in reaching out to the communities beyond the campus in
order to establish meaningful dialogue and interaction. While
this may sound abstract, the material results suggest otherwise.
My own efforts have yielded a wealth of results. In collaboration with various partners we have generated grants with school
districts that promote genuine historical analysis and content
for schoolteachers, and that also assist teachers to do program
development with their peers. There has also been the establishment of a vital and extensive professional development collaboration with the United Federation of Teachers (the New York City
Teachers' Union). This effort includes the establishment of the
Urban Educators Forum, which has already brought scholars,
researchers, community activists, and educators from across the
United States together for a sustained dialogue on urban education. The Urban Education Forum has also established a network
of support to give schoolteachers assistance with publishing their
own work and research. Other results include productive and
collaborative outreach with neighboring suburban school districts, working with them to develop programs and courses that
better serve their teachers. But the results also include internal
initiatives, some informal and "private," as it were (for example,

working together with senior and junior faculty to address issues with the administration). There are ongoing efforts and projects as well that include working with colleagues from other institutions of higher education to create, maintain, and expand a network of resistance and opportunity.

All of this work is time-consuming and can be genuinely risky, and all of it requires viewing educational leadership as a critical practice. It demands finding and working one's position in the great game of power. Augusto Boal's game offers us an opportunity to engage critically and experientially with the dynamics of power, allowing us to traverse the domain of power and locate ourselves within it. In so doing we explore not only the landscape of power, but that inner landscape that Parker J. Palmer speaks of so passionately in *The Courage to Teach: Exploring the Inner Landscape of a Teacher's Life*. In his book he tells us that he persists with this question of the inner landscape

> because it marks a seldom-taken trail in the quest for educational reform, a trail toward recovery to the inner resources that good teaching always requires. Real reform is so badly needed — and we have restructured education so often without reaching that distant dream — that we should be sending expeditionary parties down every trail we can find. (7)

Through his theater, writings and activism, Augusto Boal has offered himself as both an explorer and trail guide. By following his steps in the great game of power we can send "expeditionary parties," as Palmer wishes, safely down many of the trails (if not every one) that lead us toward discovering who we are and where else we might choose to go.

5

THE VISIBLE AND THE INVISIBLE

I am an invisible man. No. I am not a spook like those who haunted Edgar Allan Poe; nor am I one of your Hollywood-movie ectoplasms. I am a man of substance, of flesh and bone, fiber and liquids — and I might even be said to possess a mind. I am invisible, understand, simply because people refuse to see me. Like the bodiless heads you see sometimes in circus side-shows, it is as though I have been surrounded by mirrors of hard, distorting glass. When they approach me they see only my surroundings, themselves, or figments of their imagina-tion — indeed, everything and anything except me.

Ralph Ellison, *Invisible Man*

I still remember the sting I felt the first time I consciously knew that someone completely misrepresented who I was. I was very angry, but I was also really hurt — shocked and frightened might be more accurate. As a kid, I hung out with different groups. I was athletic and enjoyed playing some organized sports. I loved music and played in different bands, and I liked many of my teachers so I had lots of school activities and pals. I moved from place to place with relative ease and was welcomed by each group, even if I was not quite a bona fide member of all of them. On one particular occasion, however, an older and much bigger boy — not a musician, not a school pal, not a sports buddy, but one of the power brokers at a park I would frequent — made me a target for some reason.

I had just performed a typical adolescent stunt showing off my physical prowess. I had a really good sense of balance and was flaunting my stuff by walking the entire length of a fairly high chain-linked fence — admittedly not a particularly macho feat, although there were sharp barbs protruding at the top. I had completed my fence strutting and was basking in the momentary attention such acts sometimes allow you to garner. For that moment I was visible in exactly the way I wanted to be seen. That abruptly changed when this large body approached me from out of the crowd and told everyone that I was a faggot. As proof, he offered my just completed crowd-pleasing fence walking as evidence — what kind of expression of masculinity was "tip-toeing" across a fence? But he did not stop there, he also said that I hung out with a gay teacher, was a "faggy student-government type," and hung out with some of those weirdoes who played sissy music. For good measure he added this *non sequitur*: that I was helping Mexican farmers.[1]

I carefully considered his assault and aspersions. Being a boy and a native New Yorker in need of defending my manhood, I promptly told him to "fuck off." I was still feeling the confidence of being seen in a good light by everyone else, and was convinced that my employing the standard street response would be the end of his attack. Unfortunately, I underestimated his status within this group. As quickly as I had gotten their attention and praise, I was now transformed into a demon needing to be exorcised from their ranks. As I ran from the park being chased half-heartedly by a bunch of no longer quite so friendly acquaintances, I wanted to stop in order to tell them that he was wrong, that he distorted everything. But I kept running until I was out of sight, because I knew they would forever see only what he had described.

It is important to acknowledge that such distortions and misrepresentations occur in academia all the time. By invoking the work of Ralph Ellison, I have certainly made it easy for us to begin exploring and discussing some of the many ways in which race and racism become part of the distorting machinery operating in education today. As my retelling of this playground incident suggests, sexism, homophobia, and racism can easily be conjoined, even in illogical and forced ways (which is always the case). But my reason for recounting my moment of suffering from the act of re-vision, if I may put it that way, is to touch upon the very notion of what gets seen and unseen in educational institutions. Clearly, people of color, lesbians, gays, and transgender individuals, those with physical challenges, and working class students, among others, know all too well the various ways of being seen or not seen. And over the past thirty-plus years we have had many examples of first-person accounts of dealing with various forms of prejudice, various forms of being "re-visioned."

Despite the fact that many have written eloquently, powerfully, and persuasively about racism, homophobia, sexism, class elitism, bias against those with physical challenges, ageism, and so on, struggling against such distortions remains a daunting task. But instead of immediately starting our discussion of the notion of "the visible and the invisible" from the perspectives of race, class, and gender. I would like to continue the discussion along the lines of the preceding chapters. What I have in mind is the following: to lay out some general observations about power and visibility in academia using the insights, experiences, and examples of theorists and practitioners and offer my own analysis and opinion. These insights, experiences, and examples are, of course, tied to race, class, and gender, as we will quickly see, but I want to work from a structural analysis toward a material one, as it were, if that is an appropriate distinction at this point in history.

Addressing the structural-historical dynamic of the French university system in his book *Homo Academicus*, which I cited in Chapter 4, Pierre Bourdieu points out:

> The structure of the university field is only, at any moment in time, the state of power relations between the agents or, more precisely, between the powers they wield in their own right and above all through the institutions to which they belong; positions held in the structure are what motivate strategies aiming to transform it, or to preserve it by modifying or maintaining the relative forces of the different powers, that is, in other words, the systems of equivalence established between the different kinds of capital. (128)

To enter this "state of power relations" (the "field", as Bourdieu calls it) is to step into the great game of power discussed in the previous chapter. That is, how one is perceived within this state of power relations, how one is seen or not seen, determines where one fits in "the systems of equivalence." Regardless of how you see yourself, the existing power relations determine where you do and do not belong. In her book *Outside in the Teaching Machine*, the literary and cultural theorist Gayatri Chakravorty Spivak elaborates on this structural-historical dynamic playing itself out during a time marked by competing groups of "marginal agents" who were struggling within the "state of power relations" — that is, the university. "How could it be otherwise?" Spivak asks. After all,

> we are dealing here with the aggregative apparatus of Euro-American university education, where weapons for the play of power/knowledge as puissance/connaissance are daily put together, bit by bit, according to a history rather different than our own. One of the structurally functional ruses of this manufacture or putting-together is to give it out as the cottage-industry of mere pouvoir/savoir or the ontic, the everyday, the ground of identity. If we are taken in by this ruse, indeed propagate it through our teaching, we are part of the problem rather than the solution. Indeed, it may be that the problem and the solution are always entangled, that it cannot be otherwise. That may be the reason why persistent critique rather than academic competition disguised as the politics of difference is a more productive course. (53)

And it has been the course of "persistent critique" that critical pedagogues, from Paulo Freire to bell hooks, have been pursuing in the struggle to make education "otherwise," make it, that is, the practice of freedom. But doing so means, necessarily, that you will be looked upon (looked at) in a certain way. You will not be looked upon favorably by those dominating the "aggregative apparatus" of educational institutions. That is, you will be seen as a problem and a threat by those who *are* the apparatus — as one can argue via Bourdieu and Spivak — at any given time. Frustratingly, this has included and continues to include, as Spivak suggests, those engaged in "academic competition" disguised as doing something different, what I will here call *the studies*: queer studies, women's studies, cultural studies, etc. Even those doing interesting and important work can still get their vision clouded by the aggregative apparatus of academia, what I have been calling throughout this book the circuitry of power. Their vision impaired, they too see people and actions in distorted ways. In short, what Spivak calls "academic competition" can just as easily influence someone working in one of the academy's once "marginal" fields of study as it can influence those working in any of the traditional disciplines. Without needing to repeat some of the horror stories that have circulated over the years, it is clear that racists, patriarchs, class elitists, and other fools have operated in some of the very departments and programs purporting to study and confront these themes and issues.[2]

As I have mentioned before in this book, I made the decision to work in academia as someone committed to pursuing what Spivak calls "persistent critique." I have consequently encountered my share of being seen in a distorted fashion, even by others claiming to be committed to a critical pedagogy. Of course, I am well aware that I am not alone, that others have suffered long before I ever arrived on the academic scene, and that others have suffered more. I am proud, however, that despite a lot of pain, and some harm, I have managed to be different, managed to remain engaged in persistent critique, including self-critique. I also acknowledge that I have succeeded and thrived in academia in a number of ways. I am, for example, currently a full professor of humanities and teacher education. Many of the programs and initiatives that I directed, created, or participated in have proven to be educationally, financially, and professionally successful (by my standards as well as those of the mainstream). I say this not for self-congratulatory reasons — although as I say, I am proud of managing to be different — but because it is important to acknowledge and give testimony to more than just the bad news, the failures, and the rejections. Part of the effort to be seen otherwise — to be seen for what one is — means making yourself visible to those who suffer from the myopia that limits and distorts the vision of so many in education today.[3]

In her essay "I Don't Do Dis Here Dat Dere: A Subtext of Authority in Teaching and Learning," from the volume *I've got a story to tell* which she co-edited (and which I refer to in a previous chapter), Sandra Jackson recounts her experience of teaching an advanced placement English literature course. After the first two or three meetings, "white students were no longer attending [the] class" (23). As Jackson tells it, there was some parental

> concern about whether I was qualified to teach [the white] children what they needed to know to score high on the college admissions and advanced placement exam, and thereby not have to take introductory literature and English courses, and get into the universities and colleges of their choice. (23)

Jackson then goes on to describe another encounter some twenty years later. This time Jackson is teaching a graduate course in education and she is challenged by a White student who doubts Jackson's ability to grade her because the student sees Jackson as somehow unqualified (read, because Jackson is African American). Jackson describes her experience:

> For me an African American and woman teacher, the racial and color divide was broad — with a White student by virtue of her Whiteness presuming that I was not capable of reading her paper and commenting with authority of knowledge or credentials. How could I judge her writing and ability to communicate? After all, I was just a Black person, unable to appreciate her skill. Though she too was a female, there was no solidarity on the basis of gender. She questioned my authority

in terms of my qualifications, knowledge, and exhibited disbelief that I knew what I was talking about. (28)

The fact that this was a student "seeing" a teacher in some distorted manner and not an administrator manipulating the "state
of power relations," as Bourdieu names it, is beside the point. The
fact that this graduate student could only see her professor this
way, because of what Parker J. Palmer has identified as the "divisive structures" of educational institutions, is the point. The student's flawed vision is affirmed and maintained, if not created,
by those in positions of power, including some of Jackson's liberal
colleagues. This student's disbelief is as much a product of the
institutional racism that is still prevalent in academia as it is the
result of everything racist about her existence (academic and not)
prior to this particular face to face encounter, which sadly must
include her undergraduate education (and teachers?).

Jackson was misrecognized by this student in a certain way;
she had misidentified Jackson for reasons that had to do with the
way the state of power relations was established and maintained.
The student was misinformed — deformed, as it were, due to her
racism — about herself and the world she had been perceiving,
including how she did and did not see Jackson. Her misrecognition of Jackson is as much a matter of profound socio-historical
projection as it is a question of one's allegedly simple misperception, one's mistake of identity, so to speak (the familiar refrain,
"Oh, excuse me! Now I see; I didn't realize …" comes to mind).

Discussing a particular phase in the development of infancy
involving the formative function of the "I," the controversial
late French psychoanalyst Jacques Lacan formulates the act of

misrecognition (*méconnaissance*) in his essay "The Mirror Stage," from his collection *Ecrits*:

> This development is experienced as a temporal dialectic that decisively projects the formation of the individual into history. The mirror stage is a drama whose internal thrust is precipitated from insufficiency to anticipation — and which manufactures for the subject, caught up in the lure of spatial identification, the succession of phantasies that extends from a fragmented body-image to a form of its totality that I shall call orthopaedic — and lastly, to the assumption of the armour of an alienating identity, which will mark with its rigid structure the subject's entire mental development. (4)

Although specifically addressing a particular moment (at approximately 6 to 18 months) in the child's ego formation, Lacan's suggestion that the "drama whose internal thrust is precipitated from insufficiency to anticipation" can be useful to us here to flesh out some of the psycho-dynamics of the student's racism.

The infant experiences the dynamic of capturing an image (the mirror image of itself) and projecting a more formed and mature body, prematurely. The infant sees something more complete, more formed in the mirror, but something that is *not* the case. The infant sees something that is not there — not yet, anyway. Jackson's student engages in a structurally parallel act, only here resulting in the misrecognition of Jackson as inferior and of "seeing" herself as above and beyond the critical eye of Jackson. The similarity is in the act of misrecognition. The student, at a particular moment in her socio-historical development, sees something that is ultimately inaccurate, "a drama whose internal thrust is precipitated from insufficiency to anticipation." In this case, there is a "misinformed" formulation of one's own (embodied White) image and status based upon the (racist's) misperceived and "insufficient" image of some other. Here the "other" suffers from the "anticipated" image formed prematurely, that is, formed before the student could accurately (maturely) see what in fact she was looking at, namely *Jackson the professor*. For the student, Jackson is seen not as a qualified educator but as the untrustworthy Black poseur, based on "the assumption of the armour of an alienating identity which will mark with its rigid structure the subject's entire mental development." As Jackson puts it,

> For those who behave in this way and exhibit dismissive attitudes, I am reminded of the persistence of the color line and racial stereotyping of African Americans and others as inferior, inarticulate, incompetent, whose knowledge and skills are to be questioned. Here I share with you what I call a folk proverb which runs like this: when it comes to competence, it is for Whites to prove that they can't do something and it is for Blacks (and Others) to prove that they can. (29)

The student's behavior toward Jackson and the context in which Jackson performs her charge as professor cannot be separated. The aggregative apparatus of the Euro-American university system is at work here, and administrators who are committed to confronting and changing the conditions that produce and maintain the distorted view of such students must be engaged in a critical practice.

Just as critical pedagogy is at work in the classroom, it is important to see educational leadership as a critical practice as well. This can be achieved by a number of different means but must be predicated on an engagement with those forces and ways of seeing things that challenge and offer hope. For example, part of the reason (part of the underlying condition) for

Jackson's student seeing things the way she did relates to how she had been taught to see African Americans (and perhaps women) in general. But this particular way of seeing (or not seeing) is not just something learned before a student enters an educational institution; it is re-taught and reinforced by those dominating the hierarchies of colleges and universities in many different ways. The fact that there may be people of color teaching at a particular school does not mean that the way of seeing them is any less distorted than at a school where there are none, or less distorted than at an earlier, more racist moment in our nation's history.

The work of resisting current and residual racism can be painful and difficult work, but, as bell hooks affirms in her book *Teaching Community: A Pedagogy of Hope*:

> Once we can face all the myriad ways white-supremacist thinking shapes our daily perceptions, we can understand the reasons [why even] liberal whites who are concerned with ending racism may simultaneously hold on to beliefs and assumptions that have their roots in white supremacy. We can also face the way black people/people of color knowingly and unknowingly internalize white-supremacist thinking. (30)

Administrators are obliged to think of the larger picture: who comes to give special lectures, how does the curriculum reinforce racist stereotypes, who occupies positions of visible professional respect and competence, and so on. All of this is tied to seeing things differently and speaking a language that consistently challenges and resists the "divisive structures" of educational institutions and invigorates academia with hope instead of the professional cynicism and indifference that seems to permeate the very core of education.

As Henry Giroux argues in *The Abandoned Generation*:

> educators need to resurrect a language of resistance and pos-
> sibility, a language that embraces a militant utopianism while
> constantly being on guard against those forces that seek to
> turn such hope into a new slogan, or that punish and dismiss
> those who dare look beyond the horizon of the given. [...] It
> makes concrete the possibility for transforming hope and
> politics into an ethical space and public act that confronts the
> flow of everyday experience and the weight of social suffering
> with the force of individual and collective resistance as part
> of the unending project of democratic social transformation.
> (58)

This language must be spoken — not just by critical pedagogues
who are in the classrooms, but by administrators who view their
work as a critical practice. In order to address the distorted vision
of students, colleagues, and ourselves, we must diligently challenge ourselves to see beyond "the flow of everyday experience"
as viewed by the myopic dominating forces still controlling much
of education, from pre-K to graduate school.

The issue of racism is one aspect of the visible and the invisible in academia. There are many other reasons why someone or
some group (even a whole program or department) can be seen
one way and not another. Once again Pierre Bourdieu is helpful.
Talking about the status (value) of the different disciplines and
faculties (inside and outside) the academy, he notes:

> Although academic knowledge tends to gain social recogni-
> tion, and thereby also social efficacy, both of which increase
> as scientific values become more generally recognized (espe-
> cially as a result of technological change and the activities
> of the education system), it can only receive its social force
> from the outside, in the form of a delegated authority able
> to use socially grounded academic necessity to legitimate its

"arbitrary" social values. But this statutory authority is able to maintain the same circular relation of legitimization with an art like clinical practice, or with scholarly traditions such as theology, law or even the history of literature or philosophy, whose fundamentally social necessity resides in the last analysis in the "common opinion of scholars," itself rooted not only in a rational need for coherence and compatibility with facts, but in the social necessity of a system of objectively orchestrated dispositions and the more or less objectified and codified "arbitrary" cultural values which express it. (64)

In the United States, for example, the popularity of an academic major such as computer science, engineering, business, or forensic science can rise and fall with the economy; that is, jobs. But there are other factors of prestige and achievement at work here as well; even the popularity of a law or medical television show or Hollywood film can influence things. All of this has an impact on the size (the actual number) and status of the disciplines and their faculty. Add to this mix the distinctions, both real and imagined, among liberal arts colleges, universities, and technical and professional schools, and the status of any one discipline is up for grabs. This is so, in part, because so much can be subject to the "arbitrary cultural values" outside academia. As a result of this state of affairs, we must acknowledge that there are existing and conflicting valuations *within* an institution at any given moment in time.

For example, educational institutions of all stripes and sizes, from small liberal arts colleges to major research universities, engage in valuations that give privilege and distinction to a particular program or field of study while devaluing and undermining the very legitimacy of others. Such valuations can be based on a number of factors: (1) revenue generated (grants, tuition, donations); (2) perceived prestige (citation in a highly esteemed journal, magazine, or newspaper; an appearance as a guest or analyst on television or radio; (3) current tastes and trends (the technology obsession, moral values and current affairs — homeland security and the cost of oil); among other influences. It is the case that at a certain moment in U.S. history disciplines such as German or classics (Greek and Latin) enjoyed distinction and status, resulting in "strong" departments and wielding influence on policy and curriculum throughout academia; they no longer can claim such status. This is due, in large measure, to shifts in the geopolitical arena (suddenly Arabic is a hot language, and Chinese is being learned by every telecommunications businessperson in the United States), and the changing demographics of the student body in the United States. These modulations have made "computer graphics" and accounting among the new power brokers, even at liberal arts colleges (even a cursory look at the majors offered at traditional liberal arts colleges indicates that "professional studies" have muscled their way onto center stage).

Nor can we ignore the fact that teacher education remains as suspect as ever (even the quantitative areas of research), under assault from different fronts — public opinion, federal and local governments, corporations, and higher education itself. We have too many examples: the shutting down of the School of Education at the University of Chicago; the national trend of creating "fast-track" certification programs for change-of-career individuals to fill growing teaching vacancies but bypassing teacher education programs; and the attacks (explicit and subtle) on the very legitimacy of "education professors" who must continue to endure the stigma of being viewed by other academics as "sub-par scholars" lacking any real knowledge or expertise regarding any field of study, including education. (The creation and expansion of "charter schools" and corporations such as Edison Schools, as well as the numerous business-school partnerships, suggest things are heading in the wrong direction.)[4]

Power struggles over the status — and at times, the very existence — of a program or discipline at an educational institution make for strange and often unethical alliances and outcomes. Faculty finding themselves forced to compete for scant resources too easily fall prey to inflating their own significance — internally and beyond — while directly and indirectly dismissing the importance of others. All involved get caught up in the effort to be seen as necessary, invaluable, and important to the mission of the institution; they see each other as threat and competitor, and less and less as colleagues and educators. Everyone who has been through a budget cut or an ideological purging knows all too well the nature of this aspect of academia. There are, unfortunately, many tales and unacceptable outcomes; I want to discuss one example to further articulate the dynamic of the visible and the invisible at work in everyday academic affairs.

I am reporting, in a truncated manner, a situation that many of you have encountered directly or have witnessed from afar. The fact that it is a familiar story only suggests, to my mind, that the ideology of fatalism I spoke about in Chapter Two certainly plays a role in what is visible and invisible. I suppose it is somewhat understandable that we have grown accustomed to our myopia and confuse blurred and distorted images for the things we, in fact, do not see. And yet each revealing of things being viewed one way and not another is an opportunity to see beyond the limit that has become the norm, and to see more than our shortsightedness has typically allowed.

A senior faculty member, a full professor with many years of service at the same institution, was given substantial financial resources to develop and direct a new program. The institution's administration (including a dean and provost) deemed the program and the individual professor to be of great potential for revenue (monies generated because of grant opportunities and additional tuition) and prestige (it was considered a "cutting-edge" program). With limited funds available to support their vision, monies had to be taken from other programs viewed as less important or "on their way out." This meant that other programs and departments had to trim their budgets: cuts in release time for research and college-wide service, cuts in course overloads, cuts in the number of adjuncts resulting in larger classes, cuts in summer stipends, cuts in funding for travel reimbursements for conferences, cuts for new hires, and even cuts in supplies. Everything was scaled back in order to make the new program succeed; monies moved quickly from one place to another. Department chairs, program directors, coordinators, and administrative staff were told to cut their budgets or not request additional funds. People were understandably upset, and so began the appeals, entreaties, ultimatums, and deals.

Because the new program was viewed with such favor, adjustments had to be made throughout the institution. Sometimes people complied for the good of the institution, sometimes out of fear that they might be seen in a bad light; but in at least one case, someone said no. Although not the chair of his department, this particular well-known professor felt that his department was being short-changed, and challenged the administration. This professor threatened to leave if his department was not given the green light to recruit and hire a new faculty member, promised the previous year but now delayed until the following year. He was gone within the year, off to a place that saw him and his discipline as valuable. And his departure had its consequences, but hardly the consequences he intended. Rather than suddenly seeing their mistake and attempting to revise their plan, the administration was able to use this professor's "selfish" departure against his department. His leaving made a vacancy, one that he had publicly claimed the institution could not withstand. He was too valuable, or saw himself as such. By leaving, however, this professor inadvertently caused his department to be viewed as difficult, problematic, and ultimately weak. As those of us who have been there before know, even in cases of "devastating" losses, institutions survive — not necessarily well, but they do go on.

The administration of this institution got to frame the professor's departure as an indication of the department's unwillingness to be a team player, and used this opportunity to promote an image of the department as full of selfish, self-important, overpaid careerists who made no genuine contribution to the well-being of the institution. (The administration circulated the salaries of some of the "star professors" from that department.) So what was perhaps initiated as a legitimate if somewhat self-serving protest got "re-visioned" as nothing more than a complaint by an over-priced bag of wind, from a department that wasn't worth much anyway. The professor may have once been seen as a useful commodity, viewed as someone who could make the department and the institution more visible nationally; and the department enjoyed being seen as something important, bringing prestige to the institution and those associated with it. But things changed, and the professor and the department saw themselves one way and the administration saw them another. In the end the "aggregative apparatus" of the institution adjusted the vision of those who saw things differently — it is all about seeing things their way.

I have purposely not identified the type of program that got the support or the discipline that the professor was associated with, because it does not really matter. Of course, it matters within the given context: at a particular moment "arbitrary cultural values" influence the relative symbolic capital of a given discipline or individual at an educational institution. But the structural dynamic of being seen favorably or as insignificant can be established among a variety of agents. It does not matter who, per se; it only matters that this is an ongoing dynamic that must be seen for what it is. For example, at a business school it could easily be the case that the professor in question is a humanities professor. Originally this professor was hired as an endowed chair. An alumnus of the institution who made a fortune in the corporate world had good memories of the one philosophy course he took at the school and donated a goodly sum of money to support and expand the humanities in general, and philosophy in particular. In addition, it was implied that if this worked well more money would be donated to the school's general endowment. Despite the fact that the senior administration had neither animosity nor goodwill toward philosophy (there were no majors and only a few courses taught), they were unanimous in their decision to accept the endowed chair, with hopes of more funds to come. The once virtually invisible humanities division suddenly becomes very visible and all the machinations that go with such a hire are put into motion.

Fast-forward to the moment when a new, exciting business program can get up and running, allowing the school to remain cutting-edge. The donor has since given many times more money than the original donation for the endowed chair, and seems no longer that interested in or concerned about philosophy — he is now more attentive to the construction of a new building and business center with his name on it, a much more visible presence at his alma mater. Funds are needed, the process of cuts and reallocations begins, and the professor once viewed as important is now just a footnote in the annals of good institutional advancement strategy. Literally no one from the administration needs to see him anymore; no need for a meeting, no need to keep him or his department happy. The school has now excluded him from its field of vision.[5]

At an "arts" school it could be a science professor or department getting the short end of the stick. After all, they have no majors to speak of, and no one sees the school as a place to do science. But even at major universities (public and private), departments within divisions can fight among themselves for bragging rights and status, allowing opportunities for those from other divisions to gain attention, to move from the background into the foreground. How individuals, as well as departments and even divisions, get viewed is determined by factors that often have little to do with meaningful intellectual or social criteria, but rather are more often based on the myopia of the moment.

So far we have touched upon the notion of the visible and the invisible from a couple of perspectives. We have considered an individual (Jackson) being misrecognized by another (her student), and we have just discussed the fate of two programs and the individuals associated with them coming to be viewed as unimportant or insignificant. But certainly there are numerous examples (far too many) of other ways of being seen and not seen. One additional aspect of this dynamic that I want to discuss has to do with what work gets seen and what work remains unnoticed and devalued. I raise this issue because over the years I have experienced firsthand the fact that a lot of hard work gets accomplished but not necessarily recognized by those charged with the responsibility and power of "re-viewing" others at key moments in their careers (tenure, promotion, sabbatical, and so on).

I have also witnessed and have heard ample testimony concerning the erasure of work that was once recognized (visible) by virtue of institutional edict: this kind of work is no longer valid for this or that purpose. A classic example of this phenomenon is that of rendering previously recognized work as no longer acceptable for tenure, promotion, research release time, etc. What were once seen as legitimate and valid contributions to scholarship and community service are now "not enough."[6] What I am addressing is the reality that a lot of people do good and valuable work that takes time, effort, skill, and generosity of spirit yet remains unseen, and as a result they do not get the professional recognition they deserve. Some of this has to do with the nature of the work, some with the dispositions of those who are doing the seeing (or rather the not seeing).

Some work is, by nature, less visible. One example is time spent with a student or a colleague attempting to resolve some issue or intervene on behalf of someone else — that is, working toward making someone else's life better. Another example is certain committee work (some might say all committee work) — the sometimes endless meetings given over to policy debates, curriculum and program approvals, and so on. In addition, school teachers are often forced to volunteer their time to programs and activities before and after school, spending time tutoring and dealing with parental issues that are beyond their responsibility, but they do it nevertheless. Many different types of work can go unnoticed and unappreciated; the invisible effort need not be rewarded or financially compensated. This makes for "good" administrating. What's interesting to note is that certain people get a lot of attention, rewards and compensation, and a lot of visibility, despite doing very little or low-quality work. Don't get me wrong; I am a firm believer in the statement, "Working hard may be admirable, but working well is better."

Unfortunately, many who work hard and well are often overshadowed by those who barely work, and when they do they often do it poorly, requiring additional work by unacknowledged others. Much more effort is needed to create fair and just criteria for evaluating the work people do. And there must be greater effort to require that those individuals and committees doing the "reviewing" look for and see the things that they typically choose not to see. If the aggregative apparatus, as Spivak calls it, remains blind to the type of work that is vital to viewing education as the practice of freedom, then the ethical and political futures of educational institutions here in the United States are doomed to do little more than reproduce students with the shortsighted goal of becoming successful consumers and shareholders, students who suffer from the same myopia that accounts for the many distorted views that abound today and are seen as real insights.

Administrators committed to leadership as critical practice may not single-handedly be able to cure the myopia that distorts who people really are, or the nature and quality of their work. But by being committed to confronting and challenging the existing distortions, by seeing the importance of critically engaging others to reconsider their perspective, administrators can play the important role of being genuine leaders and not just people managing the status quo. This involves the hard and valuable work of assisting individuals, departments, and whole communities to see and be seen as they are, for what they are, beyond the distorting pettiness of academic competition, beyond the distorting projections of racism, sexism, class elitism, and ageism, beyond the distorting selfishness that blinds one to the noble efforts and good work of others.

6

DIALOGUE AND BUILDING COMMUNITIES OF PARTICIPATION

It is only the category of multiplicity, used as a substantive and going beyond both the One and the many, beyond the predicative relation of the One and the many, that can account for desiring-production: desiring-production is pure multiplicity, that is to say, an affirmation that is irreducible to any sort of unity.

Gilles Deleuze and Felix Guattari
Anti-Oedipus: Capitalism and Schizophrenia

In his passionate and insightful book, *The Community of Those Who Have Nothing in Common*, philosopher and cultural theorist Alphonso Lingis cautions:

Every discourse among interlocutors is a struggle against outsiders, those who emit interference and equivocation, who have an interest in that the communication not take place. But in the measure that communication does take place and that statements are established as true, it designates outsiders as not making sense, as mystified, mad, or brutish, and it delivers them over to violence. (135)

Long before the events of September 11, 2001, "we" were living in a world marked by the polarizing ideology of us versus them. This perspective has been around for centuries — remember the Greeks and the "barbarians." And long before the establishment of the Department of Homeland Security, the desire to produce and maintain the unity (and security) that allegedly comes from belonging to a community has animated and motivated much of what defines the United States — the Civil War was about many things but it was, above all else, about saving the Union. The imagery and mythology of a United States of America has been, perhaps from before the declaration of its existence, working to produce (seemingly, at all costs) something it needed to justify its future; namely, a past it never really had. From the purity of the Pilgrims to the predestiny of the western expansion, the story of America had been told by those creating a history that would lay the foundation for what was yet to come, the great promise of this democracy.

Those of you who have read this far are probably asking, "What does any of this have to do with educational leadership as critical practice?" But you might rightly be asking whether or not this is directly related to the *everyday* task of running a program or being a dean, never mind being the head of a high school physical education department. For me the answer is a simple, "Yes, of course it is." Part of the reason why I say yes so quickly and unequivocally is due to the fact that much of what has come to be known as the culture wars revolves around the very notion of what the United States is all about — its history, present, and future. This is important for educators generally, and for administrators who see themselves as leaders, because "school," from kindergarten to graduate school, is, perhaps, one of the places where our democracy stands the best chance, as the philosopher Richard Rorty puts it, of "achieving our country."[1]

For some this may sound a bit melodramatic and decidedly pre-postmodern, but as I hope to argue here, educators are, as Paulo Freire notes, "cultural workers." If this is so, then everything educators do, including assuming administrative roles and responsibilities, must be done within the context of attempting to achieve our country. Otherwise, teaching is little more than participating in the current neoliberal effort to produce *smart* and *independent* consumers. As Henry A. Giroux demands in *The Abandoned Generation*:

> Educators need to be clearer about how power works through texts, representations, and discourse, while at the same time recognizing that power cannot be reduced to the study of such representations. Changing consciousness is not the same as altering the institutional basis of oppression; similarly, institutional reform cannot take place without a shift in consciousness capable of recognizing the very need to reinvent the space of collective struggle and the strategies for constructing an inclusive democracy. (55)

Giroux is right on the mark when he tells us that educators need to be "clearer about how power works," that this includes how power works "through texts, representations, and discourse," and that there is a need to recognize "that power cannot be reduced to the study of such representations." Without meaning to undermine the significance of studying "such representations" — and they must be studied — too many very sophisticated readers and critics have, intentionally or not, confined their work within the clearly delineated borders of the classroom or lecture hall. This, in and of itself, may not be all that bad; however, there are too many who are confusing it with (and representing it as) "altering the institutional basis of oppression." As a consequence, many political progressives have come to criticize the academic left, the "cultural left," for its neglecting traditional power struggles (the economy, labor, taxes, the welfare state, etc.) and its ineffectiveness in bringing about change in the material existence of the lives of the world's poor and oppressed.

In his book *Achieving Our Country*, Richard Rorty identifies this distinction (this division of labor, as it were) in a number of different ways. Here he notes that:

> the cultural Left does not think much about what the alternative to a market economy might be, or about how to combine political freedom with centralized economic decisionmaking. Nor does it spend much time asking whether Americans are undertaxed, or how much of the welfare state the country can afford, or whether the United States should back out of the North American Free Trade Agreement. When the Right proclaims that socialism has failed, and that capitalism is the only alternative, the cultural Left has little to say in reply. For it prefers not to talk about money. Its principal enemy is a mind-set rather than a set of economic arrangements — a way of thinking which is, supposedly, at the root of both selfishness and sadism. This way of thinking is sometimes called "Cold War Ideology," sometimes "technocratic rationality," and sometimes "phallogeocentrism" (the cultural Left comes up with fresh sobriquets every year). It is a mind-set nurtured by the patriarchal and capitalist institutions of the industrial West, and its bad effects are most clearly visible in the United States. (78-79)

Although admittedly sarcastic and dismissive of the cultural left's political efficacy (in the material sense of the phrase), Rorty rightly notes an important issue: the need to address directly social injustice in the United States and do something about it.[2] It is very much within the context of doing something toward the goal of achieving our country that I want to advocate critical pedagogues, and others sympathetic to this movement, pursue the work of administration, work that can alter the institutional basis of oppression, at least within educational institutions.

But this means working together with others from all corners of academia and having the courage, fortitude, and skill to do so. It is one thing to be elected chair of a department, or to be appointed dean of a school or division or director of a program, and participate in the maintenance of the status quo. It is, however, quite another thing to work with the disparate groups who inhabit academic institutions, and often inhibit any meaningful change in academia due to the issues raised in previous chapters: the ideology of fatalism and, the culture of fear and academic competitiveness, among other factors. As the sociologist Zygmunt Bauman puts it in his book *Community: Seeking Safety in an Insecure World*:

> To stand up against the status quo always takes courage, considering the awesome forces gathered behind it — and courage is a quality which intellectuals once famous for their obstreperous radicalism have lost on the way to their new roles and "niches" as experts, academic boffins or media celebrities. One is tempted to take this slightly updated version of *le trahison des clercs* for the explanation of the puzzle of the learned classes' resignation and indifference. (125)

Taking a position of responsibility and power, as we have discussed, is done within the larger context of the structure and dynamics of power *already* in operation. To ignore this context is to act irresponsibly — that is, uncritically. In order to identify, confront, and alter the existing institutional basis of oppression, or, as Parker J. Palmer has called them, the "divisive structures" of educational institutions, we need a strategy for dismantling those structures, and we need to work with others to enact this change. Individual action is vital and necessary, but, alas, not sufficient for change — unless others participate and join in the movement, the shift, from the way things are to the way things ought to be, we end up, as Alphonso Lingis suggests, being seen "as not making sense, as mystified, mad, or brutish." This is why, as bold as it may sound, educational leadership as critical practice is a moral imperative: *it is what we should do, together.* It is also why such leadership requires a genuine vision of the way things can be; it is not nearly enough to be a "good" or "competent" administrator — managing to be different demands something beyond that, something other than business as usual. But if we are going to participate in educational leadership as critical practice, we must be clear-sighted and of one mind about engaging others, of talking *with* others. We must be committed to working with the communities of others who exist, in their multiplicity, but are not yet dialogically engaged with us, not yet the positive force that can come together to effect change.

In speaking about community in his book *The Courage to Teach*, Parker J. Palmer frames the issue this way:

> Community cannot take root in a divided life. Long before community assumes external shape and form, it must be present as seed in the individual self: only as we are in

communion with ourselves can we find community with others. (90)

His notion of community is predicated on a certain understanding of human interaction beginning with, as he puts it, "the inner-landscape of a teacher's life." Palmer's distinctly non-postmodernist stance on this should not lead us to reject his position as naïve. Though using a language and model that are consistently spiritual, and "privileging" some terms and ideas over others (who doesn't?) in a manner that would be fodder for any graduate student working from a postmodernist perspective, Palmer offers us an authentic (one of his favorite words) and what I believe to be a useful starting point for thinking about working together with others.

The reason I find Palmer useful here is because, as he describes it:

> The model of community we seek is one that can embrace, guide, and refine the core mission of education — the mission of knowing, teaching and learning. We will find clues to its dimensions at the heart of the image of teaching that most challenges me: to teach is to create a space in which the community of truth is practice. (94)

His model, "one that can embrace, guide and refine the core mission of education," is a model that is consistent with educational leadership as critical practice — that is, of creating space for critical consciousness to develop and be engaged by faculty, students, and administrators. But one needs to know who one is and how one wants to live — ethically, justly, and freely — in order to "guide and refine."

In her book *Teaching Community: A Pedagogy of Hope*, bell hooks approaches this issue from a similar, but politically more explicit, perspective. Reflecting on the consequences of some of her White male students giving up a "racialized gendered notion of authority," bell hooks tells us:

> One of the most positive outcomes is the commitment to "radical openness," the will to explore different perspectives and change one's mind as new information is presented. Throughout my career as a democratic educator I have known many brilliant students who seek education, who dream of service in the cause of freedom, who despair or become fundamentally dismayed because colleges and universities are structured in ways that lead them away from the spirit of community in which they long to live their lives. More often than not, these students, especially the gifted students of color from diverse class backgrounds, give up hope. They do poorly in their studies. They take on the mantle of victimhood. They fail. They drop out. Most of them have had no guides to teach them how to find their way in educational systems that, though structured to maintain domination, are not closed systems and therefore have within them subcultures of resistance where education as the practice of freedom still happens. Way too many gifted students never find these subcultures, never encounter the democratic educators who could help them find their way. (48)

Part of the reason why these students "never encounter the democratic educators" is due to the fact that these educators are themselves subject to the "divisive structures" that hide them or otherwise make them unavailable. "Democratic educators," as bell hooks identifies them, are too often not hired, not tenured, not promoted, and therefore not available. The "subcultures of resistance," as bell hooks calls them — the communities of others, as I have identified them — are necessary if education is to assist in the effort of "achieving our country."

As bell hooks argues, "Most of them have had no guides to teach them how to find their way in educational systems." She is advocating a strategy, therefore, that seeks to "embrace, guide, and refine the core mission of education." This is a strategy, however, that will not succeed unless those in positions of leadership manage to be different — that is, create real dialogue with those who are different, meaning those who are committed to education as the practice of freedom.

In his *Pedagogy of Freedom*, Paulo Freire talks about what it takes to be ready for dialogue:

> In my relations with others, those who may not have the same political, ethical, aesthetic, or pedagogical choices as myself, I cannot begin from the standpoint that I have to conquer them at any cost or from the fear that they may conquer me. On the contrary, the basis of our encounter ought to be a respect for the differences between us and an acknowledgement of the coherence between what I say and what I do. It is in openness to the world that I construct the inner security that is indispensable for that openness. It is impossible to live this openness to the world without inner security, just as it is impossible to have that security without taking the risk of being open. (120)

Freire, like hooks, adds a more explicit political dimension to the position expressed by Parker J. Palmer, but is nevertheless consistent with Palmer's view of what kind of person it takes to engage in genuine dialogue and building alliances. It takes a person, according to Palmer, "who has grace, the flowing of personal identity and integrity into the world of relationships." This includes the generosity of spirit to be open to encountering others — as Freire puts it, "those who may not have the same political, ethical, aesthetic, or pedagogical choices as myself." Those of us attempting to approach educational leadership as critical practice must embrace the practice of being open to those who in fact have different histories and trajectories — that is, different lived experiences and different desires.

Too often administrators come to view differences solely within the closed context of fighting battles — winning them and losing them — not with openness, with the possibilities of establishing meaningful dialogical relationships with those others we encounter in our work. "The person," Freire tells us,

> who is open to the world or to others inaugurates thus a dialogical relationship with which restlessness, curiosity, and unfinishedness are confirmed as key moments with the ongoing current of history. (121)

But so many times we are not open in this way because of the demands of finishing things by the deadline. We lose our curiosity about what others are thinking or doing, because of what we need to tell them in order to accomplish what we have before us. We also shy away from the restlessness of such dialogic encounters because of an understandable desire for closure — so many things hanging over our heads. Dialogue opens things up, and dialogue can only occur when we have the openness that Freire, Palmer, and hooks talk about throughout their work — the openness to engage with others in a mutually respectful manner. This is why an administrator needs more than competence, unless it is the sort of competence that one speaks of when we identify a way of being in the world, of being open, a way of being that Freire takes as a given.[3]

Being this way, of course, comes from commitment and conviction, not from promotion and appointment. Leadership as critical practice is that sort of engagement that critical pedagogues have practiced in their classrooms, their scholarship, their professional encounters, and their lives outside academia over the years — namely, the ongoing work of education as the practice of freedom.

Henry A. Giroux powerfully lays out this position in his book *Border Crossings: Cultural Workers and the Politics of Education.* Concluding an interview in the book, Giroux tell us:

> That's why [critical] pedagogy is both exhilarating and dangerous. It's one of the few forms of cultural politics that cannot simply be consigned to academia. Its central questions of ideology and politics ask how people take up what they take up; that is, how they participate in, produce, and challenge particular ways of life. The issue is not simply how people are inserted into particular subject positions but also how they create them. To raise that question is automatically to engage the language of specificity, community, diversity, difference and the struggle for public life. (161)

Giroux stakes out an intellectual and political mode of existence that is both "exhilarating and dangerous" for lots of reasons, including the fact that it makes us confront the tough questions, questions that ask us to consider and reconsider how we are in the world. Anyone in a position of leadership in education must also question the nature of our participation and our role in producing (or reproducing) a particular way of life. And as Giroux tells us, to ask such a question "is automatically to engage the language of specificity, community, diversity, difference and the struggle for public life."

This is how educational leadership as critical practice is linked to the cultural, social and political life inside and outside academia. This is the good news, and also the bad news (for those who would have it otherwise). Although many administrators at educational institutions live in denial or consciously attempt to suppress the communities of others that *are* those institutions, the need for acknowledging these different participants is essential, both for the existential condition that Giroux affirms and for the life of the educational institutions that they lead. Unfortunately, the way many administrators and institutions respond to this need typically falls far short of a critical perspective. This is why administrators who are engaged in the critical practice of leadership will find ways to open up to those around them and work with them to ask the difficult questions about how they are in the world and what they are willing to do about it.

As I said earlier on in this chapter, managing to be different means having the commitment, courage, generosity, and skill to engage those who are not necessarily the folks you would first think of working with to move ahead. But it is the communities of others that we must attempt to have dialogue with if we are serious about being competent, in the best sense of that word, at our work, the work of education as the practice of freedom. Getting different groups to participate in asking the type of question that Giroux tells us is the heart and soul of critical pedagogy is the work of educational leadership. It is a leadership that consciously seeks out those who inhabit the educational institution, and a leadership that initiates dialogue in the manner that Freire describes. It is a type of leadership that manages to be different in both form and content, because it is a leadership predicated on being open to what others have to contribute to education as the practice of freedom, not what they do that poses obstacles to that goal. Institutionally, this means consciously setting out to create communities of participation.

In their article, "Designing the Social Architecture of Participation in Large Groups to Effect Organizational Change," Thomas N. Gilmore and Charles Barnett tell us:

It is in this context that we want to explore "the social architecture of participation" — creating the scaffolding that can
support the necessary thinking that could result in structural
changes. The social architecture of participation may be a
model of the project-oriented, permanently changing organization structure of the future. We are particularly interested in
the design of settings that bring together large heterogeneous
groups, what Weisbord has termed "the whole system in the
room." (535)

Although Gilmore and Barnett are considering the organizational
structure of mostly high- and middle-ranking managers at hos-
pitals, their article sheds light on the issue of creating communities of participation that I have been pursuing at educational
institutions.

While the overlap is in fact interesting, and some of their strategies for gathering information and solutions are useful, it is
primarily the notion of designing "the social architecture of participation" that I want to discuss. As Gilmore and Barnett note,
"The culture of any organization takes its shape from the front
line task." (538) If we accept (and advocate) Freire's notion of
"education as the practice of freedom," then our "front line task"
is teaching a critical pedagogy. But as we have discussed in the
previous chapters, not everyone in academia views education this
way, and as a result, for many the front line task can range from
making more money to controlling others, to many things other
than engaging in a critical pedagogy. So it is important to keep in
mind that part of what is necessary to help create communities of
participation is the alignment of the task, which in turn means
working with others towards gaining a critical perspective — in
other words, dialogue.

One of the things that many of my colleagues often point out about me is that I know everyone. This is of course not true; I do, however, make a genuine effort to know as many of the stakeholders of a given project, program, or group as I can. Part of this, to go back to Bourdieu, is a matter of my "disposition," but it is a strategic move — I embrace the real value of dialogue — that enhances my chances of meeting good people to work with me. By acknowledging others who sometimes get pushed into the background, I get the opportunity to engage in dialogue with thoughtful, talented, and committed individuals who are looking to participate more fully or seeking collaborators in education as the practice of freedom. Many times, these encounters occur not at some general rally calling for the radicalization of education, but at some rather mundane bureaucratic gathering or meeting. Sometimes dialogue begins not so much as a direct result of talking about education as from engaging in conversation about the day-to-day politics of the institution where we work.

For example, there have been many occasions, especially with those whose stated politics drastically differ from mine, where we have fallen into dialogue about some college-wide policy, budget cut, pay issue, teaching load, or other business issue. What could start and end with a very limited topic, I try to extend and broaden by inquiring, as Giroux put it:

> How people take up what they take up; that is, how they participate in, produce, and challenge particular ways of life. The issue is not simply how people are inserted into particular subject positions but also how they create them (161).

That is, it is not only possible but, in fact, quite natural for people to become interested and engaged in dialogue about that which has an impact on them. The goal is, however, as Paulo Freire notes in *Pedagogy of Freedom*, to move beyond the complaint about this or that, and to transform the angry and disgruntled attitudes into committed, positive positions and actions. Freire advises:

> One of the basic questions that we need to look at is how to convert merely rebellious attitudes into revolutionary ones in the process of the radical transformation of society. Merely rebellious attitudes or actions are insufficient, though they are an indispensable response to legitimate anger. It is necessary to go beyond rebellious attitudes to a more radically critical and revolutionary position, which is in fact a position not simply of denouncing injustice but of announcing a new utopia. Transformation of the world implies a dialectic between two actions: denouncing the process of dehumanization and announcing the dream of new society. (74)

A perfectly valid jumping off point is bonding with a colleague who has been wronged. That moment of communication, of dialogue, however, needs to go beyond the immediate concern (sometimes quite trivial, sometimes very profound). This is how we can begin to develop a "social architecture of participation." We can build upon the foundation of frustration and anger, of the desire to vent, to rebel against those in charge. We can move beyond the superficial and construct an ongoing dialogue that involves the interlocutors in the important act of questioning, as Giroux describes it, "how they participate in, produce, and challenge particular ways of life."

This is how educational leadership as critical practice can genuinely engage colleagues from the many sectors of academia, from the different communities of others — as Alphonso Lingis might have us consider it, from those who have nothing in common — to participate in something they can choose to share. This is how we begin to build up the social architecture of participation; *we do so by being genuinely open to dialogue and the concerns of others.* In that space of openness we create the foundation for an architecture of participation because there is real bedrock upon which to build. Whatever else transpires, those who experience real dialogue are much more willing to continue to build upon the foundation of mutual exchange. In doing so they begin to participate in constructing a more cogent critique of their own dehumanization and begin to announce the possibility, the dream of a different way of life. This is the work of educational leadership as critical practice, of managing to be different. This is so because in the process of questioning, in the process of establishing and maintaining dialogue, we enable those who have the willingness to rebel to transcend their anger and engage in education as the practice of freedom, including their own freedom. Communities of participation are built upon such exchanges and transformations, upon dialogue.

For those who have experienced the power of dialogue and the solidarity it can bring about, the increase in the level of participation is not that surprising, though it is always impressive. For those who have not, all of this might sound a bit corny at best, and perhaps little more than idle chatter at worst. Yet, time and again, I have witnessed the building of communities of participation as a direct result of dialogue. It has been, and continues to be, dialogue that offers the opportunity to challenge the power and the ideology of academia that deceives us into thinking that we are doing something that we are not. As Václav Havel writes in the collection of essays, *The Power of the Powerless*:

> Ideology is a specious way of relating to the world. It offers human beings the illusion of an identity, of dignity, and of morality while making it easier for them to part with them. As the repository of something "supra-personal" and objective, it enables people to deceive their conscience and conceal their true position and their inglorious *modus vivendi*, both from the world and from themselves. (28-9)

And it is genuine dialogue that confronts such deception in the very act of mutual exchange. We reveal to each other who we are in dialogue and build communities that participate in removing the illusion of dignity with the genuine possibility of achieving it.

The fact that engaging in dialogue might strike some as too simple a method for gaining understanding and the momentum needed for change ought not to discourage us from doing this simple thing. bell hooks tells us in *Teaching to Transgress*:

> To engage in dialogue is one of the simplest ways we can begin as teachers, scholars, and critical thinkers to cross boundaries, the barriers that may or may not be erected by race, gender, class, professional standing, and a host of other differences. (130)

Learning the value of dialogue as a simple means of communication, of mutual sharing, allows us the opportunity to develop communities of participation, because the participation is unfolding through dialogue itself. The act of recognizing someone as worthy of your time and attention is the first act toward designing the social architecture of participation. Building upon this foundation can (and necessarily does) look different in different settings. The particular issues, the materials with which you have to build, are different, even if familiar. The fact that you "already had this conversation" at some other place, with other people, should not prevent you from starting the dialogue anew. Administrators who engage in educational leadership as critical practice engage in dialogue. They work to build communities of participation in order to address those obstacles that get in the way of education as the practice of freedom, and to speak out loud about achieving it. To be in dialogue is to be already establishing communities of participation, communities working toward the noble goal of "achieving our country."

POSTSCRIPT:

OF POMO ACADEMICUS

Inspired by Jacques Derrida ... deconstructionists hold that all literature is empty of meaning. Whereas structuralists try to find linguistic parallels and contrasts in texts, deconstructionists labor to discover ingenious, and sometimes bizarre, contradictions which render the work "radically incoherent."

Dinesh D'Souza, *Illiberal Education*

Now "everyday language" is not innocent or neutral. It is the language of Western metaphysics, and it carries with it not only a considerable number of presuppositions of all types, but also presuppositions inseparable from metaphysics, which, although little attended to, are knotted into a system.

Jacques Derrida, *Positions*

I can still remember my dismay at the cultural brouhaha and moral outrage in the United States over the alleged influence of French "post-structuralist" thought of the 1970s and 1980s. It was a mostly retroactive response that only emerged in full force during the late 1980s and early 1990s, and is today known mostly as the culture wars. Chief among the concerns of those (over)reacting to this "invasion" was the work of the philosopher Jacques Derrida, but other French intellectuals — most notably

Michel Foucault — also made the hit lists of social conservatives and the religious right. They were all lumped together with feminists, queer theorists, and multiculturalists as "postmodernists." Interestingly enough, however, and long before these perceived threats to the stability of academic law and order, there were French thinkers who enjoyed the status of American celebrity: Jean Paul Sartre, Simone de Beauvoir, Albert Camus, and Gabriel Marcel to name a few. Granted the "existentialists" arguably caused a popular culture sensation not quite on par with the successful marketing of hip-hop to mainstream America (read suburban White America). But it was a really huge thing by *intellectual* standards — every hipster was wearing a beret, holding a cigarette between her or his thumb and index finger, drinking a cappuccino or sipping a vermouth and uttering the phrase, "Oui, mais, c'est trés absurd."

The impact of "postmodernism," however, worked its way primarily through academia in the United States and did not find a mass-market audience. If you weren't a college or a graduate student (almost anywhere) in the humanities and arts, chances are you knew very little, if anything, about postmodernism until architects and clothing designers started "deconstructing" everything and anything they could get their hands on. Before that moment of commercial visibility, outside of academia, the term deconstruction was pretty much the concern of ambitious (and typically clever) English professors, a few oddball law professors, and just about every Romance language professor looking to teach "theory." Surprisingly to many, one of the university disciplines that did not embrace Jacques Derrida was philosophy. Departments of philosophy, at the time, were very much enamored with Anglo-American "analytic" philosophy (they still are) and pretty much ignored Derrida altogether. At the height of his academic career, Jacques Derrida, who was a professor of the history of philosophy at the Ecole Normale Superieure in Paris, never held a visiting professorship in philosophy during the 1970s and 1980s in the United States. He was always the guest of various literature departments.

To be sure, there were philosophers in the United States who were very interested in Derrida and postmodernism, but very few departments focused on what in professional philosophy usually gets called contemporary continental philosophy. During the 1970s and 1980s there was essentially only one department in the United States that could legitimately claim to be "continental," the State University of New York at Stony Brook — it is where I earned my Ph.D. But even philosophers committed to working in continental philosophy were further divided into subgroups, so that the actual number of people really engaged with the work of Derrida, as opposed to the work the German phenomenologist Edmund Husserl or his famous student Martin Heidegger or other contemporary continental philosophers was very modest, when compared to the large numbers of literature professionals attending the Modern Language Association's annual meetings during that same period. Despite how relatively few people actually knew or read the philosophical tradition that Derrida's work focused on, many people came to view his subtle, complex, esoteric and original analysis as the latest "method" by which to do — or as was often the goal, undo — their own discipline or work. By the time this method played itself out, even famed film director Woody Allen was "Deconstructing Harry" (not a bad film by the way, but...). The point is, that by the time deconstruction made its way into the mainstream (academic and elsewhere), what is, in fact, a very complicated and rich philosophical critique was pretty much reduced, in the most banal sense, to a "method" that just about anyone could mimic, if not quite understand. As a result, the backlash to Derrida and postmodernism had to do more with the fears, misunderstandings, and orthodoxy of those who were sounding the death knell for Western civilization than with a philosophically informed response to Derrida et al.

Most conservative cultural critics, and a few from the left, ultimately were reacting to the explosion of new topics and genres of study that questioned what was once the "certainty" of the epistemological and moral foundations of many academic disciplines and those of the dominant social, cultural, and political practices throughout the United States. Soon the debate was framed this way: you are either a patriotic, faithful (read Christian), heterosexual capitalist or a national security threat, and a relativist, sexual pervert, anti-capitalism anarchist. All of this, it was claimed was due to the "dangerous" thinking spreading throughout academia. Summing up his argument in his book *The De-Valuing of America: The Fight for Our Culture and Our Children*, former Secretary of Education William J. Bennett claims:

> Many of America's intellectual elite perpetrated a doctrine of *de facto* nihilism that cut to the core of American traditions. While the doctrine never fully took hold among most Americans, it did make significant inroads. A lot a people forgot, and many others willfully rejected, the most basic and sensible answers to first questions, to questions about what contributes to our social well-being and prosperity, what makes for individual character and responsibility, and what constitutes a "good society." (255-56)[a]

Bennett along with many other "traditionalists" equate the very act of questioning the foundations of a culture to rejecting all beliefs and principles, especially if such questioning challenges a particularly sanitized and romanticized image of the United States. Such questioning, even if done in an ivory tower and not on the streets, was and still is viewed, as Bennett asserts in his subtitle, was a threat to the future of "our culture and our children." Much of what is called postmodern is automatically considered part of this questioning. Any challenge to the longstanding dominance of a euro-centric or patriarchal reading of the history of the United States is a problem for those whose political and moral values have stood unshaken, at least from where they stand (on top). In his collection of public lectures, *Prophetic Thought in Postmodern Times*, noted Princeton University professor Cornel West emphasizes the significance of this interrogation:

> This is very important as we shall see when we talk about multiculturalism and eurocentrism, because it means from the beginning we must call into question any notions of pure traditions or pristine heritages, or any civilization or culture having a monopoly on virtue or insight. Ambiguous legacies, hybrid cultures. By hybrid, of course, we mean cross-cultural fertilization. Every culture that we know is a result of the weaving of antecedent cultures. Elements of antecedent cultures create something new based on that which came before. (4)

But such "talk about multiculturalism and eurocentrism" threatens the stability of a narrative that has been circulating in and out of schools and universities in the United States since their establishment. Such "talk" is an example of what D'Sousa asserts are attempts by deconstructionists to "labor to discover ingenious, and sometimes bizarre, contradictions which render the work 'radically incoherent'" (178). Here, of course, "the work" is the history of the United States as told from only one perspective, one way of seeing things—as historian Howard Zinn puts it in his book *A People's History of the United States*, "the telling of history from the standpoint of the conquerors and leaders of Western civilization" (22).

Those of us who arrive at colleges and universities already engaged in such talk—talking otherwise about the way things are — are typically viewed as problems. As I discussed in this book, we "mess things up." In many cases, there is a sense of muted outrage: "after all *we* gave you this job, and now you are telling us that we are racist, sexist, homophobic, supporting corporate globalization, and participating in a mythology that harms students." And when the reply is, "well, actually, yes," the muted outrage gets really loud. The fact that the newly hired professor may include herself or himself in the critique of such things is beside the point; it is not heard. Where things were once settled they are now rendered "radically incoherent." The fact that this has been going on for more than thirty years does not change the dynamic; those who disrupt the status quo, those who demand that something more be done about those "divisive structures" of academia, *are* a threat to the tranquility and security of the established order. But they also represent the greatest possibility for change and engaging in education as the practice of freedom.

This is why it is important for those who are leaders, for those who do talk differently, to gain administrative positions in order to help create and sustain communities of participation. Such academics can help shift efforts away from those merely trying to maintain the past to rigorously and honestly trying to understand it, and create genuine communities of teaching and learning. There must be a move away from the historical *Homo Academicus* to the radically evolved *Pomo Academicus*. I am purposely (and admittedly playfully) using the title of Pierre Bourdieu's book examining the "French academic" as the name of the academic as traditionally understood (with the good connotations as well as the problematical aspects discussed in this book). *Pomo Academicus* is my name for the appearance and proliferation of the postmodern pedagogue that represents a political and temperamental (dispositional, as Bourdieu might put it) shift away from the traditionally constituted university educator. This is an *evolutionary* shift or movement, something that cannot be stopped — like all of evolution, it happens. Academics, more and more, have been confronting the realities of the university under the old regime, under the influence of a particularly narrow narrative about and engagement with the world and their work. As critical pedagogues have been asserting for years (and before them feminists and other civil rights activists), there can no longer be a disconnect between theory and practice.

In an interview titled "Truth and Power" in the collection of interviews and writings *Power/Knowledge*, Michel Foucault frames the shift this way:

> A new mode of the "connection between theory and practice" has been established. Intellectuals have got used to working, not in the modality of the "universal," the "exemplary," the "just-and-true-for-all," but within specific sectors, at the precise points where their own conditions of life or work situate them (housing, the hospital, the asylum, the laboratory, the university, family, and sexual relations). This has undoubtedly given them a much more immediate and concrete awareness of struggles. And they have met here with problems which are

specific, "non-universal," and often different from those of the proletariat or the masses. And yet I believe intellectuals have actually been drawn closer to the proletariat and the masses, for two reasons. Firstly, because it has been a question of real, material, everyday struggles, and secondly because they have often been confronted, albeit in a different form, by the same adversary of the proletariat, namely the multinational corporations, the judicial and police apparatuses, the property of speculators, etc. This is what I would call the "specific" intellectual as opposed to the "universal" intellectual. (126)

Pomo Academicus is the intellectual that gets "specific" and moves away from the tendency of *Homo Academicus* to universalize, to claim the "just-and-true-for-all" and to maintain the status quo. This specificity can cause problems for the current order of things.

In the conclusion to *The Abandoned Generation*, Henry A. Giroux suggests that such specificity must include:

> what it means to deepen and expand the struggle for establishing pedagogical approaches and movements that can be used to mediate the fundamental tension between the public values of higher education and the commercial values of corporate culture, on the one hand, and fight against the devastating assaults waged against the welfare state and other public goods on the other. If the forces of corporate culture are to be challenged, educators must also enlist the help of diverse communities, interests, foundations, social movements, and other forces...(195)

Giroux and other critical pedagogues have been getting specific for quite some time, as they continue to engage education as the practice of freedom. But the neoliberal influence — never mind the non-ending presence of and interference by the hard-core right — makes such a practice difficult at best, and professionally, if not personally, dangerous at worst. Critical pedagogy has embraced postmodernism, in part, because of its re-evaluation and re-consideration of things that are understood as given and immutable. As Derrida has rightly argued, the narrative that has been claiming to be objective "is not innocent or neutral."

This does not mean that every word uttered by some pompous *Homo Academicus* is devoid of meaning and is incoherent; it is just more likely than not that what is uttered is meaningful and coherent in ways that are not recognized or acknowledged by the uncritical person who made the statement. It is equally the case that there are a good number of people who see themselves as *Pomo Academicus* when they are, in fact, no less pompous or uncritical, no less "knotted into a system," as Derrida suggests, than *Homo Academicus*. But this does not negate the significant difference between *Homo* and *Pomo Academicus*. The difference may seem negligible to those looking in from a distance, but for those engaged in the struggle to be different, for those managing to be different, the difference is as real as any "truth" posited by those in charge. As I have argued throughout this book, taking such a position matters.

In their co-authored book, *Postmodern Education*, Stanley Aronowitz and Henry A. Giroux explain why taking a postmodern position leads to controversy and upsets the gatekeepers of Western culture. Talking of the debates and fights over education during the Reagan-Bush era, Aronowitz and Giroux point out that

> any position that questioned the utter rationality of the canon
> or indicated that the canon signified something other than
> the progressive achievements of the human mind was blas-
> phemous. Here the distinction between progressivism and

> postmodernism in education becomes most stark: unlike conservatives who blame the victims for their failure to meet established educational standards, the progressives want to make room for the excluded within the established culture; in contrast, postmodernism asserts no privileged place, aside from power considerations, for the art works, scientific achievements, and philosophical traditions by which Western culture legitimates itself. (13)

This does not mean that postmodernists see no difference between a "false" and "true" claim about the nature of things, just that even the "true" claims have no "privileged place." Every claim needs to be understood within the context of power considerations, every claim gets re-evaluated and re-considered. This position often gets under the skin of those who want to extend the domain of privilege, the domain of "the unquestionable" to some very questionable propositions forwarded as scientifically grounded or true (creationism, for example). Oddly enough, it is not that postmodernists simply or cynically fall prey to the claim, "well if nothing is privileged, than creationism is as valid as evolution." It is a much more complicated and complex situation, namely nothing is privileged and everything is contextualized by power considerations.

Instead of simple answers that ignore "difficult" aspects of a question or issue, the postmodern pedagogue is ethically obligated to push on, to ask the hard questions and risk altering the status of what was once taken as true and fixed. (*At some point in history, this was called science.*) Criticism of educational institutions and practices is not a call for a leveling of civilization, but instead an attempt to become rigorous about what gets to be called worthy or valuable to our well-being and future. Such a critical position is by definition always in motion, always re-considering and re-thinking what is offered or taken as "given." As Aronowitz and Giroux put it:

> Central to the notion of postmodern educational criticism is the need for educators to rethink the relations between the centers and the margins of power. That is, this view of educational criticism must not only call into question forms of subordination that create inequities among different groups as they live out their lives but also challenge those institutional and ideological boundaries that have historically masked their own relations of power behind complex forms of distinction and privilege. (194)

Accordingly, postmodern educational criticism is ethically and politically charged in ways that makes it "dangerous" to any and all who refuse to acknowledge the work that is necessary to unmask "their own relations of power."

The courageous position of challenging those who claim to know, with certainty, things that require more work and explication than the simple assertion that "I know it to be true" is not new. In many ways it is an ancient position, one that is the heart and spirit of the Western tradition. In his moving reconstruction of the trial of Socrates (in *Euthyphro, Apology, Crito* translated by F.J. Church), Plato has Socrates explain his "impious" and "immoral" behavior to the Athenian court at his (Socrates') trial. Telling of his encounter with the oracle of Delphi and his consequent effort to understand its meaning and test its validity, Socrates explains to his jurors:

> For a long time I was at a loss to understand his meaning. Then, very reluctantly, I turned to investigate it in this manner: I went to a man who was reputed to be wise, thinking that there, if anywhere, I should prove the answer wrong, and meaning to point out to the oracle its mistake, and to say, "You

said that I was the wisest of men, but this man is wiser than I am." So I examined the man—I need not tell you his name, he was a politician — but this was the result, Athenians. When I conversed with him I came to see that, though a great many persons, and most of all he himself, thought he was wise, yet he was not wise. Then I tried to prove to him that he was not wise, though he fancied that he was. By so doing I made him indignant, and many of the bystanders. So when I went away, I thought to myself, "I am wiser than this man: neither of us knows anything that is really worth knowing, but he thinks that he has knowledge when he has not, while I, having no knowledge, do not think that I have. I seem, at any rate, to be a little wiser than he is on this point: I do not think that I know what I do not know." Next I went to another man who was reputed to be still wiser than the last, with exactly the same result. And there again I made him, and many other men, indignant. (26)

Socrates' efforts to seek out the meaning of the oracle and its truth led him to engage with others who claim to be wise, to be the wisest about things. His position, his challenge to their claim and status, was met with indignation. To move about within the city of Athens and call into question the legitimacy and authority of those in positions of power could not, and ultimately did not, go unpunished. In the case of Socrates, he was condemned to death; he was deemed a moral and social threat to the children and culture of Athens, the future of their democracy. Socrates had many opportunities to conform, to hold back and to shut up, but he could not and would not. He was obligated to resist, to transgress, and to be different as those he questioned insisted on their wisdom and authority. It was a power struggle in the most ethical sense: it was about the willingness, the generosity, of someone to ask aloud the questions no one wanted to hear. At that moment in history the response was a definitive rejection and negation of such questioning.

Pomo Academicus is at this moment in history able to (obligated to) ask some important questions about things that many have taken for granted, and wish to ignore or simply assert as true. In asking the annoying questions, the threatening questions, *Pomo Academicus*, like Socrates, moves things, shifts them around from the privileged places they have occupied for so long. In challenging the artificial and tenuous security of things as they have been, those postmodern educators who engage in educational leadership as critical practice necessarily take risks, and are greeted with indignation. But in managing to be different they also successfully meet the challenge of teaching and learning, of engaging in education as the practice of freedom, as an ongoing act of becoming. Whether or not our nation, our democracy, is any better prepared than the Athenians to hear such questions, to have a dialogue with those who challenge us to reconsider and rethink what we take as true, we can only hope. That is, we must hope. Hope is a pedagogical as well as political position about the future, about the promise of what is to come. It is what we must dream about.

In his *Pedagogy of Hope*, Paulo Freire tells us:

> Dreaming is not only a necessary political act, it is an integral part of the historico-social manner of being a person. It is part of human nature, which, within history, is in a permanent process of becoming. (91)

Those postmodern pedagogues who have the (political) imagination to dream otherwise, who have the fortitude and skills to embrace educational leadership as critical practice, find ways of managing to be different at every turn. They find ways of asking the risky questions and demanding that we all strive to engage education as the practice of freedom. They are, as Freire asserts, dreaming, hopeful of the future.

Pomo Academicus spem somniat.

ABOUT THE AUTHOR

Ron Scapp is the founding director of the Graduate Program in Urban and Multicultural Education at the College of Mount Saint Vincent, the Bronx, where he is a professor of humanities and teacher education. He holds a Ph.D. in philosophy. In addition to other publications, Scapp is the author of *Teaching Values: Critical Perspectives on Education, Politics and Culture* (also with Routledge). He is a senior associate of the United Federation of Teachers' Urban Educators Forum and a Fellow of the Education Policy Studies Laboratory at Arizona State University. Scapp has collaborated with bell hooks and others on numerous projects. He is the series editor of *Dialogue with Teachers* and series co-editor of *Hot Topics: Contemporary Philosophy and Culture* and *Positions: Education, Politics and Culture.*

NOTES

Introduction

1 For a more complete discussion concerning my views on this particular issue see my *Teaching Values: Critical Perspectives on Education, Politics and Culture.*

2 Even though there are many "change of career" individuals and others who can get their certification to teach or administrate through some alternative means, just about everyone still has direct experience with higher education, and typically some interaction with a teacher education program, even if in some abridged fashion.

Chapter Two

1 Regarding Freire and postmodernism I direct the reader to my essay, "The Subject of Education: Paulo Freire, Postmodernism and Multiculturalism," in *Mentoring the Mentor : A Critical Dialogue with Paulo Freire.* Despite viewing postmodernism from a different (more positive) perspective than Freire, I see the connection between his work and that of many postmodern thinkers and critics as important and, to my mind, useful.

2 Because so many people in academia, on some level or another, believe that things are fixed, there is a resignation, if not an out-

right willingness, that allows them readily and often unapologetically to participate in the ideology of fatalism.

3 One immediately thinks of the national sensation over and backlash to professor Ward L. Churchill of the University of Colorado and his "incendiary" comments concerning the attacks on 9-11. (See *New York Times* article, 2/11/2005.) As a New Yorker who lived through that awful day, I find the comments and analysis a bit facile and sophomoric, and, perhaps more importantly, insulting to the memory of those who died or were injured or otherwise traumatized but who are not legitimately or accurately described in his essay, in which he referred to those at the World Trade Center as "technocrats" and "little Eichmanns," alluding to the Nazi Adolf Eichmann. (Clearly he wasn't thinking about the many working-class service and maintenance people and restaurant workers, among other non-Eichmanns who worked at the World Trade Center and died that day.) I do not, however, view his words or position, in any way, as unpatriotic or subversive. And we ought not to focus just on this nationally televised character assassination; we must remember the various schoolteachers across the nation who were reprimanded and, in some cases, even forced from their classrooms for merely questioning our going to war with Iraq.

4 It will suffice, for my purposes, to simply note that "training" is not the same as educating. That is to say, training usually means little more than indoctrinating students in the type of (non-)thinking and (non-)acting that is synonymous with the ideology of fatalism. At the risk of insulting colleagues across the country, most teacher education and education leadership programs do, in fact, merely train, and do not educate their students.

5 For an example of such an exchange I direct the reader to the *Dialogue with Teachers* series published by the United Federation of Teachers Professional Development Program, the UFT/Teacher Center.

Chapter Three

1 For an excellent discussion of this issue see Alex Molnar's book, *School Commercialism: From Democratic Ideal to Market Commodity.*

² See my "Taking Command: The Pathology of Identity and Agency in Predatory Culture," in *Education as Enforcement: The Militarization and Corporatization of Schools*, edited by Kenneth J. Saltman and David A. Gabbard.

³ As I have been saying throughout this chapter, there are lots of ways of doing this: from fighting for meaningful curriculum reform, to working with colleagues concerning critical pedagogical strategies, to supporting and assisting those who need backup; the work is there, to be determined by you and your colleagues. I have attempted to do things internally and with external partners. Here the examples are not the point; the point is having the willingness and skill to navigate and negotiate your way through the "world as it is" in order to help create a world as it ought to be.

Chapter Four

¹ I would like to express my gratitude to Deborah R. Geis for introducing me to the work of Boal and for her challenge to me to consider the performative dimensions to teaching.

Chapter Five

¹ At the time, I was president of my sophomore class, and although I played electric and acoustic bass, mostly for rhythm and blues bands, some friends played early music (lutes, flutes, and all). I did hang out with different teachers, some of whom were gay, and I did some work for the United Farm Workers Union, then just getting up and running — Si Se Puede.

² Please do not misunderstand me as trying to debunk or undermine the significance of "the studies" as I have here called them — I myself was the director of such a program. But it would be dishonest and unhelpful to suggest that everyone associated with programs and disciplines dealing with race, class, and gender are *ipso facto* free of racism, class elitism, and sexism, or are somehow immune from "academic competition" and the distorted vision it can create.

³ Because I want to respect the privacy of people, I will use previously published accounts to make my case, or, when necessary, alter some of the facts of as yet unpublished testimony of what is being discussed here.

⁴ I direct the reader to Kenneth J. Saltman's book *The Edison Schools: Corporate Schooling and the Assault on Public Education*.

⁵ In his book *Experimental Phenomenology: An Introduction*, Don Ihde provides readers with a succinct and useful guide to some important and related issues concerning perception, or what is seen. As he notes, "The maxim Edmund Husserl coined to characterize phenomenology was, 'To the things themselves'" (29). Of course, getting to the things themselves, as phenomenology asks us to do, requires a rigorous and systematic method of seeing things as they appear. I recommend Ihde's book to those who are tempted to experiment with how they see things and to consider new perspectives and means of describing what they see.

⁶ Although it should be mentioned that when the "aggregative apparatus" works for you or against you, you and your work are seen as acceptable or not regardless of the stated requirements. For example, if it had been a long established requirement for a particular department that a published book is needed in order to earn tenure, but the "agents" in power do not want you, they will have their narrative all set to go. "Yes, you published a book, but it was at a third-rate press." "True, your book was published at a first-rate press, but it got bad reviews." "OK, you got great reviews for a book published at a first-rate press, but your student evaluations stink." "Yes, great book, great reviews, great student evaluations, but not enough evidence of committee work." And the opposite: "Yes, his book was published at a 'second-tier' press, and it got mixed reviews, but what originality!" And so on; people see what they want and then force their view on everyone.

Chapter 6

¹ Oddly enough — not, by the way, ironically, for those of you who follow this debate — Richard Rorty has written a number of important books, including *Achieving Our Country*, that I think are useful for those of us who view ourselves as postmodern pedagogues. I say this because the book that announced Rorty's

affiliation with postmodern thinking, *Contingency, Irony and Solidarity*, is, I think, philosophically wrong about much of what gets called postmodern philosophy (Nietzsche, Heidegger, and Derrida). I am, however, in agreement with Rorty on some political issues about which he has argued consistently and, to my mind, cogently over the years. He is a "liberal," which is a problem, but he believes in political action, and he is committed to democracy and the idea that our country still has promise.

2   Elsewhere (see my "On the Practicality of Practical Philosophy," in *Studies in Practical Philosophy*, Vol. 4, Issue 2, 2004), I have been critical of the very "desire" to act, to do something. As I argue, "I believe that the reinvigorated desire to be useful, in philosophy, is partly the result of the backlash to postmodernism, that was alluded to earlier. For a time, critics from the left as well as the right may have viewed postmodern thought as little more than a distracting encumbrance slowing down moral and political action; however, it has quickly become identified as the ideological obstacle preventing any action. This, they claim, is harmful to our existence as a nation" (69). But these comments are directed toward the issue of philosophical thought and action. To be fair to Rorty, even though I disagree with him philosophically about what he calls "identity politics" and the "politics of recognition," the value of his criticism here is genuine and useful.

3   As the philosopher Martin Heidegger asserts in his *What Is Philosophy?* (translated by Wilde and Kluback, in the College and University Press edition): "Philosophy is *episteme tis*, a kind of competence, *theoretike*, which is capable of *theorein* [speculating], that is, of being on the lookout for something and of seizing and holding in its glance what it is on the lookout for" (57). It is this notion of "competence" that is perhaps useful here.

Chapter 7

1   I have used this quote before in Teaching Values and use it again here because of how well it highlights the debate. For a more thorough discussion regarding postmodernism and the "threat" to American education, I refer the reader to "When the Truth is Gone: Teaching in an Age of Certainty" in *Teaching Values*.

REFERENCES

Aronowitz, S. and Giroux, H. *Postmodern Education: Politics, Culture, and Social Criticism*. Minneapolis: University of Minnesota Press, 1991.

Bauman, Z. *Community: Seeking Safety in an Insecure World*. London: Polity, 2000.

Bennet, W. *The Devaluing of America: The Fight for Our Culture and Our Children*. New York: Summit Books, 1992.

Boal, A. *Games for Actors and Non-Actors*. New York: Routledge, 1992.

---, *Theatre of the Oppressed*. New York: Theatre Communications Group, 1985.

Bordo, S. *Twilight Zones: The Hidden Life of Cultural Images from Plato to O.J.* Berkeley: University of California Press, 1997.

Bourdieu, P. *Homo Academicus*. Trans. Peter Collier. Stanford: Stanford University Press, 1990.

---, *Language and Symbolic Power*. Ed. and introduced by John B. Thompson. Cambridge: Harvard University Press, 1994.

---, *The Field of Cultural Production*. Ed. Randal Johnson. New York: Columbia University Press, 1993.

Collins, J. *Good to Great*. New York: HarperBusiness, 2001.

Deleuze, G. and Guattari, F.A. *A Thousand Plateaus*, Trans. Brian Massumi. Minneapolis: University of Minnesota Press, 1987.

---, *Anti-Oedipus*, Trans. Robert Hurley et al. Minneapolis: University of Minnesota, 1983.

Derrida, J. *Positions*. Trans. Alan Bass. Chicago: The University of Chicago Press, 1982.

Dostoevski, F. *The Grand Inquisitor on the Nature of Man.* Trans. Constance Garnett. Indianapolis: The Bobbs-Merrill Company, 1975.

D'Souza, D. *Illiberal Education: The Politics of Race and Sex on Campus.* New York: The Free Press, 1991.

Ellison, R. *The Invisible Man.* New York: Vintage Press, 1972.

Foucalt, M. *Language, Counter-memory, Practice.* Ed. Donald Bouchard. Ithaca, NY: Cornell University Press, 1981.

---, *Writings,* Ed. Colin Gordon. New York: Pantheon Books, 1980.

Fraser, N. *Unruly Practices: Power, Discourse and Gender in Contemporary Social Theory.* Minneapolis: University of Minnesota Press, 1989.

Freire, P. *Pedagogy of Freedom.* Lanham, MD: Rowman and Littlefield, 2001.

---, *Education for Critical Consciousness.* New York: The Seabury Press, 1973.

---, *Pedagogy of the Oppressed.* New York: Continuum, 1992.

Gilmore, R. and Barnett, C. "Designing the Social Architecture of Participation in Large Groups to Effect Organizational Change." *The Journal of Applied Behavioral Science,* 28.4 (December 1992).

Giroux, H. *Impure Acts: The Practical Politics of Cultural Studies.* New York: Routledge, 2000.

---, *The Abandoned Generation: Democracy Beyond the Culture of Fear.* New York: Palgrave, 2003.

---, *Border Crossings: Cultural Workers and the Politics of Education.* New York: Routledge, 1993.

Goodman, R. *World, Class, Women: Global Literature, Education and Feminism.* New York: Routledge, 2004.

Havel, V. et al. *The Power of the Powerless.* Armonk, NY: M.E. Sharpe, 1985.

Heidegger, M. *What is Philosophy?* Trans. J. Wilde and W. Kluback. New Haven: College and University Press, 1956.

hooks, b. *Teaching to Transgress: Education as the Practice of Freedom.* New York: Routledge, 1994.

Jackson, S. and Solis, J. *I've Got a Story to Tell: Identity and Place in the Academy*. New York: Peter Lang, 1999.

Kimball, R. *Tenured Radicals: How Politics has Corrupted Our Higher Education*. Chicago: Elephant Paperbacks/Ivan R. Publishing, 1988.

Kohl, H. *I Won't Learn From You*. New York: The New Press, 1999.

Kozol, J. *Amazing Grace: The Lives of Children and the Conscience of a Nation*. New York: HarperCollins, 1996.

---, *Savage Inequalities: Children in American's Schools*. New York: Crown Publishing, 1991.

Lacan, J. *Ecrit*. Trans. Alan Sheridan. New York: Norton and Company, 1991.

Lingis, A. *The Community Of Those Who Have Nothing In Common*. Indianapolis: Indiana University Press, 1994.

McLaren, P. *Critical Pedagogy and Predatory Culture: Oppositional Politics in a Postmodern Era*. New York: Routledge, 1995.

Macedo, D. *Literacies of Power: What Americans are not Allowed to Know*. Boulder, CO: Westview Press, 1994.

Machiavelli, N. *The Prince*. Trans. G. Bull. New York: Penguin Press, 1985.

Marx, K. *The Economic and Philosophic Manuscripts of 1844*. Ed. Dirk Struik. New York: International Publishers, 1973.

Palmer, P.J. *The Courage to Teach: Exploring the Inner Landscape of a Teachers' Life*. San Francisco: Jossey-Bass Publishers, 1998.

Penha, J. and Azrak, J. *The Learning Community*. New York: Paulist Press, 1975.

Plato, *Euthyphro, Apology, Crito*. Trans. F. J. Church. Indianapolis: Bobbs-Merrill Education Publishing, 1980.

Rorty, R. *Achieving Our Country*. Cambridge: Harvard University Press, 1997.

Saltman, K. J. Collateral Damage: Corporatizing Public *Schools – A Threat to Democracy*. Lanham, MD: Rowman & Littlefield Publishing, 2000.

---, and Gabbard, D. *Education as Enforcemnt: The Militarization and Corporatization of Schools*. New York: Routledge, 2003.

Scapp, R. *Teaching Values: Critical Perspectives on Education, Politics and Culture.* New York: Routledge, 2003.

Sedgwick. E. *Epistemology of the Closet.* Berkeley: University of California Press, 1990.

Sergiovanni, T. *Moral Leadership: Getting to the Heart of School Improvement.* San Francisco: Jossey-Bass Publishers, 1992.

Spivak, G. C. *Outside in the Teaching Machine.* New York: Routledge, 1993.

West, C. *Prophetic Thought in Postmodern Times.* Monroe, ME: Common Courage Press, 1993.

X, Malcolm. *Malcom X Speaks.* Ed. George Breitman. New York: Grove Press, 1966.

Zinn, H. *A People's History of the United States.* New York: Harper and Row, 1980.

INDEX

A

new power brokers, 92
notes, 137–138
persistent critique, 83, 84
popularity of academic major, 91
resisting racism, 89
state of power relations, 82–83, 86
status of disciplines, 90, 91, 93
student racism, 85–87
valuations to fields of study, 91
way of being seen, 81
way of seeing, 89
Invisible Man, 79
Ivory tower questioning, 123
I Won't Learn from You: And Other
    Thoughts on Creative
    Maladjustment, 45–46

J

Jackson, Sandra, 55, 85
Jordan, Jose Solis, 55
Junior faculty, 7
Just-and-true-for-all, 125, 126

K

Kimball, Roger, 3
Knowledge, market value of, 58
Kohl, Herbert, 46, 72
Kozol, Jonathan, 44

L

Labor, division of, 104
Lacan, Jacques, 86
Language and Symbolic Power, 26
Leader
    -follower structure, 12
    leadership limited to, 11
Leadership
    celebrity, 2
    communities of, 14
    models of, 11
    notion of, 14

published philosophy of, 2
    vision, 106
Learning
    experiences, game of power and,
        72
    mission of, 4
    not-, 73
Lingis, Alphonso, 101, 115
Literacies of Power, 8
Literacy tutor, 18

M

Macedo, Donaldo, 8
Machiavelli, Niccolo, 1
Making a mess, 54, 59
Malcolm X, 1
Marginal agents, 83
Marx, Karl, 26, 60
Master tutor-counselor, 19
McLaren, Peter, 10, 14
Messing things up, 36, 40, 124
Metaphors, 13
Methodology bandwagon, 8
Militant Labor Forum, The, 1
Militaristic model, 44
Mini-school, 24
Misrecognition, 86–87
Misrepresentation, 79, 81
Model(s)
    business, government's growing
        interests in using, 57
    corporate, notions of freedom in,
        58
    leadership, 11
    militaristic, 44
Modern Language Association, 121
Moral Leadership, 8
Multiculturalism, 3, 123

N

Neoliberalism
    antifederalist aspect of, 39, 41